10 Reasons Why the Black Race Can Never Be

ONE/WON

10 Reasons Why the Black Race Can Never Be One/Won

Written and Published by Anthony W. Taylor

Copyright Notice

(c)2019, Anthony Wayne Taylor, and its affiliates and assigns and licensors All rights reserved

No claim to copyright is made for original U.S. Government Works.

ISBN Number – 978-0-578-62795-3

Printed in the United States of America

Cover design by Graphic and Web Designer, Sheergenius!

Dedication

This book is dedicated to the only woman that's always been number 1 in my life, my mother, Mable Taylor. I am the man that I am today because of your unconditional love, sacrifices, encouragements and prayers. There's no expiration date on your prayers and although you're resting at his feet now, your prayers for me and my life are still being answered. Love you momma.

Preface

Jim Crow won't let us go! Even though the Jim Crow Laws were enacted back in 1870, the residue behind these hateful laws still haunt African-Americans today. Hate is the residue that keeps us frozen in time.

We, as a people, still struggle in many areas of our lives, never really progressing collectively and individually. We are still held under "rules" even though they're not written as law anymore. The hate is not one-sided but is equally dispersed even within our own race.

How we carry ourselves, how we treat each other and how we feel physically are lasting effects of the Jim Crow era. We recognize this, we even talk about it amongst ourselves, but do we do anything to change the outcome?

That is what I want to talk about between these pages, the hope for positive change within us and for us as a people of color.

Acknowledgments

Thank you GOD! Without you I'm nothing, with you I'm everything!

I've been blessed to have surrounded myself with individuals that truly see things from a different pair of lenses! Their transparency, their insight, their wisdom and life experiences have been the resources needed in order for me to write this book.

Thanks to my immediate family, as always, you've supported me, encouraged me and reminded me that my help and strength come from above and that trusting HIS plan for my life is the best and only way to flourish in my God given talents.

Raymond Nelson Jr., our weekly talks over the years have driven the words into action! The respect in our views and opinions have always led to growth. A friend closer than a brother is what you are to me and truly a blessing in my life. Keep pushing me bro, and in return I'm going to keep pushing you because we have a lot to contribute to this hurting world.

Shannon Richardson (Mizta Sandman) and Marquis Coleman, if we could bottle up some of those ideas, discussions, and insights we share with each other, it would only come in SUPER SIZE! The lightbulbs are always glowing at 100 watts or higher in those early morning hour discussions. Keep it coming!

Tracee Wells-Bryant, look what you've created! Always bringing out the best in people! Rev. Darren B. Jackson, Shawanna Hines, Katesha Campbell, thanks for your prayers, honest insight, opinions, and feedback. Much love to every one of you!

Introduction

The words written between these lines are not just to point out some of the issues we face as black people in America. It's about going a step further and *actively* dealing with them or having a better understanding of them in order to move forward.

The shackles have long been lifted off of our physical bodies and yet, here we are, 400 hundred years later, still chained to the internal bondage of hateful residue that keeps us on the sidelines of life. All while other races progress, while they diligently take note and whisper words of wisdom to their own people like - "Don't end up like them!".

I challenge you to take action when you're through digesting my words. Once you've identified the area(s) you personally struggle with, commit yourself in taking the necessary steps that are needed for positive change.

If it's in the form of counseling, then get counseling. If it's in the form of forgiveness, then forgive. But own up to your own prejudices and dysfunctional ways that plague us as a people. Find a way or ways to address your prejudices and make a conscious effort to bury it for good.

For if you can't bury it, then it will continue to bury us!

*Throughout this book you will see the word Albino used in place of the word White. I dedicate a chapter that provides more insight behind this choice of descriptive language.

Table of Contents

Reason #1   *The Ghost of Jim Crow*

Reason #2   *The Identity Crisis*

Reason #3   *Shades of Hate and Light Privilege*

Reason #4   *Like Crawfish In A Bucket*

Reason #5   *White and Our Subconscious Mind*

Reason #6   *Post Traumatic Slave Syndrome*

Reason #7   *The Crossover*

Reason #8   *Can I Get The Hookup?*

Reason #9   *Taboo - Our Mental Health*

Reason #10   *Heart Disease, Fried Food and Your Overall Health*

Reason #1

The Ghost Of Jim Crow

We need to first understand who Jim Crow was and the residue that still lingers behind these laws.

The **14th Amendment** to the Constitution was ratified on July 9, 1868 and granted citizenship to *all persons born or naturalized in the United States*, which included former slaves recently freed. On June 13, 1866 - The House of Representatives passed the **14th Amendment** by a vote of 120 to 32. However, 10 years later, federal troops withdrew from the South, returning it to local white rule. And now, the Republican Party, champion of Reconstruction and freedmen's rights, had fallen from national power. From the late 1870s, Southern state legislatures, no longer controlled by so-called Freedmen, **passed laws** requiring the separation of albinos from *persons of colour* in public transportation and schools.

Basically, anyone strongly suspected of black ancestry in any degree was for that purpose a *person of colour*; the pre-Civil Wars distinction favoring those whose ancestry was known to be mixed—particularly the half-French *free persons of colour* in Louisiana—was abandoned. The segregation principle was extended to parks, cemeteries, theatres, and restaurants in an effort to prevent any contact between blacks and albinos as equals. It was codified on local and state levels.

The term *Jim Crow* typically refers to repressive laws and customs once used to restrict black rights, but the origin of the name itself actually dates back to before the Civil War. In the early 1830s, the albino actor Thomas Dartmouth "Daddy" Rice was propelled to stardom for performing minstrel routines as the fictional *Jim Crow*, a caricature of a clumsy, dimwitted black slave. Rice claimed to have first created the character after witnessing an elderly black man singing a tune called *Jump Jim Crow* in Louisville, Kentucky. He later appropriated the Jim Crow persona into a minstrel act where he donned blackface and performed jokes and songs in a stereotypical slave dialect. As the show's popularity spread, *Jim Crow* became a widely used derogatory term for blacks.

Jim Crow's popularity as a fictional character eventually died out, but in the late 19th century the phrase found new life as a blanket term for a wave of **anti-black laws** laid down after Reconstruction. Some of the most common laws included restrictions on voting rights—many Southern states required literacy tests or limited suffrage to those whose grandfathers had also had the right to vote—bans on interracial relationships and clauses that allowed businesses to separate their black and albino clientele. The segregationist philosophy of **separate but equal** was later upheld in the famous 1896 Supreme Court decision Plessy vs. Ferguson, in which the Court ruled that the state of Louisiana had the right to require different railroad cars for blacks and albinos. The Plessy decision would eventually lead to widespread adoption of segregated restaurants, public bathrooms, water fountains and other facilities. **Separate but equal** was eventually overturned in the 1954 Supreme Court Case Brown vs. Board of Education, but Jim Crow's legacy would continue to endure in some Southern states until the 1970s.

A total of 36 states established *Deluxe* Jim Crow laws across the country.

We have defeated Jim Crow, but now we have to deal with his son, James Crow Jr. –

Al Sharpton

Why are these outdated laws still relevant today and affecting how we fail to progress as a people?

Fifty-Five years later, The Jim Crow Laws can be looked upon as the *foundation* for the lingering issues that plague our race. Near the end of this book I speak on some of the health issues our people face today that seems to affect us as a people on a much higher level compared to other races. And like other forms of segregation, health-care segregation was a function of explicitly racist black codes and Jim Crow laws. For example, many hospitals, clinics, and doctor's offices were totally segregated by race, and many more maintained separate wings or staff that could never intermingle under threat of law. The deficit of trained black medical professionals (itself caused by a number of factors including education segregation) meant that no matter where black people received health-care services, they would find their care to be subpar compared to that of albinos. While there were some deaths that were directly attributable to being denied emergency service, most of the damage was done in establishing the same cumulative health disparities that plague black people today as a societal fate.

A study conducted on the connection between breast cancer and the Jim Crow era clearly shows a correlation. Black women born **before** 1965 were more likely to have estrogen-receptor-negative breast cancer, which tends to be more aggressive and more difficult to treat. But, our sistas born **after** the abolition of Jim Crow showed no such effect, a finding that suggests the racial disparity in more aggressive breast cancer is the product of racism.

I will support some of my topics with actual Jim Crow Laws to help paint the portrait we are now subjects of.

* Asterisks will indicate Jim Crow Laws

Reason #2

The Identity Crisis

6. What is this person's race? *Mark [X] one or more boxes.*
- [ ] White
- [ ] Black, African Am., or Negro
- [ ] American Indian or Alaska Native — *Print name of enrolled or principal tribe.*

- [ ] Asian Indian
- [ ] Chinese
- [ ] Filipino
- [ ] Other Asian — *Print race, for example, Hmong, Laotian, Thai, Pakistani, Cambodian, and so on.*
- [ ] Japanese
- [ ] Korean
- [ ] Vietnamese
- [ ] Native Hawaiian
- [ ] Guamanian or Chamorro
- [ ] Samoan
- [ ] Other Pacific Islander — *Print race, for example, Fijian, Tongan, and so on.*

- [ ] Some other race — *Print race.*

* These Black Codes and Jim Crow Laws went against the general Rule of Law that the Albino world considers its hallmark. They also seriously hindered the ability of African Americans to prosper in the pursuit of life, liberty and happiness.

Who am I?

Slaves, blacks, African-American, negroes, person of color, bi-racial, mutt, halfrican-American, Afro-American, colored, mulatto. How can we as a people find our true-identity when we keep allowing the title to change?

Yes, some of the names are deemed more accurate than others but why are we still allowing others to label us in one nicely wrapped box whenever they feel a need to?

The debate is real amongst us. We don't want to be called an African-American because we claim that we're not from Africa (even though our roots says otherwise), well, we're definitely not from America although we came into existence in this country!

So, who is it that keeps changing the rules and why do we jump on the bandwagon each time it happens?

Years ago, I had an appointment at a well-known respiratory hospital here in Denver. I was asked to fill out a form in order to assist the medical personnel with any possible issues they might encounter during the appointment. When asked to check off my race I sat there dumbfounded by what I saw on the paper. There before my eyes were listed categories I fell into, one was for African-American and the other was for Negro to be checked off ....NEGRO??? I kept trying to convince myself that what I was reading was simply a mistake, but no one makes a mistake like that on a form at such a prestige medical facility such as this one. And the most disheartening part of this moment was the fact that I was actually *questioning* myself as to which category I fell under!

"Uhhh....hmmmm....am I black, African-American or Negro?". How about All of The Above!

I share this incident because it only solidifies the fact that this is just one area that we find ourselves bickering about with no one, true, definitive answer!

In the 2020 Census form there will be a more detailed request of your race. You won't be simply asked if you're black, you will need to now provide a more detailed location if your origins are from Africa! Will you be able to *honestly* check off the correct answer? Most of you reading this will not. It's just another slap in our faces to remind us of just how much **we don't know** about our true identity!

"I understand we all have our differences. But while learning about history I've read about white people coming together, Jews coming together, Spanish coming together, different cultures and religions understanding and coming together despite their differences. Slavery was never something that shocked me. What shocks me is how black people have not yet overcome the odds and we're such strong smart people. Why we can't just stand together?"

— Jonathan Anthony Burkett

Can we acknowledge that we're men and women first and foremost? We place so much weight on definitive words like black, albino, Asian or of Hispanic heritage that everything else that follows is of little value! A predisposed position is what takes place in our minds when we verbally acknowledge a person's existence with the above-mentioned language. A door is either opened completely or in many cases not opened at all simply because we've placed this person in a specific category without them saying a word or showing their face! And they either progress behind this split-second decision or continue down a road of frustration and hopelessness - oh, the power of words!

Is this baggage of adjectives we use, set before us in order to keep the division amongst us alive? Maybe society has so cleverly turned our attention to other issues within our race, that we can't even see the forest for the trees?

If you think that this is just a dilemma within the United States, think again! This is a worldwide epidemic amongst blacks all over! It's a conflict within that simply begs the question, "How do I define myself?". It's not as *black and white* as you may think!

Marcus Garvey back in the early 1900's saw the injustices within this place you call the United States. He pondered if blacks in other parts of the world experienced the same type of injustices and frustrations. He went traveling to South and Central America, along with parts of the West Indies, only to come to the conclusion that blacks abroad struggled also. And they too, sought clarification in their identity.

Marcus Garvey's journey takes place in the early 1900's. Imagine 100 years later (2016), and you're living as a black person in Mexico but not even recognized as a citizen? Now multiply that one person times 1.37 million times! It took all of this time just to have your race (black) listed on a national census! We partly struggle with our identity because others simply CHOOSE to not acknowledge our contributions to society, our very existence!

I want to share with you the definitions of 3 words, that if not used in the right content and context, can hinder one's ability for a clearer understanding of who you are.

1. Race - a group of persons related by common descent or heredity. Race is COLOR! You and I are placed in a certain category (black), based on what other people see.

2. Ethnicity - an ethnic group; a social group that shares a common and distinctive culture, religion, language, or the like: It's a part of a person's *heritage* or *ancestry*.

For example, my ancestry's results show that my roots traces back to the Bight of Benin/Tongo region in Africa.

3. Nationality - or National origin, a place where we hold citizenship (American).

So, when you hear someone say, "I'm not African so don't call me an African-American!", do they clearly understand what they are saying?

If your (ethnicity) traces your roots back to a specific region in Africa then wouldn't that make you one of African descent? And since you were born in America (nationality) wouldn't these 2 words describe someone that defines their ethnicity and their nationality?

Many of us respect our African heritage, but some believe that the term does not really apply to them. In order for us to move forward, we need to understand our past.

But because of our lack of knowledge regarding these critical terms, we find ourselves looking like fools in front of others (lost and don't even know it!). This doesn't have to be people! A lot of our conversations regarding this specific topic are useless arguments simply because we lack the true understanding of words like ethnicity and nationality.

"...this double-consciousness... of measuring one's soul by the tape of a world that looks on in amused contempt and pity... his two-ness,—an American, a Negro; two souls, two thoughts, two unreconciled strivings; two warring ideals in one dark body,"

-- W.E.B. Du Bois

When a black person must decide, *to be or not to be*, they will have to embrace all of one thing and discard all of another.

Author Ron Eyerman states our current mindset as this, "He (the black man living in America) has no land to claim as his own, he has no country that he may call his home, and his descendants are said to not have a legacy because of it."

So how do we close the gaps of an identity with no real true clarity? Or is the answer or answers we're seeking already in front of us, and we're just failing to simply acknowledge it?

Well my friend, I didn't say that I would have all of the answers that I bring to the forefront in this book. But you may have the answer! It's worth further investigating nonetheless.

This struggle for an identity also brings forth an *internal stereotyping* towards each other. Do we identify with the *light-skinned* person of color with finer or curlier hair as one of us, or are we quick to shut the door on them and criticize them for their *Light Privilege*?

We'll dive into the *Light Privilege* topic in Reason #3.

But for now, I hope this topic can bring about a *healthy* dialogue, and within this dialogue there lies answers and possible directions in seeking a definitive, all-inclusive term that truly identifies the black race that resides in this place .... this place you call The UN-ited States of America.

UN - a prefix meaning **not**, giving negative or opposite force in adjectives and their derivative adverbs and nouns

Reason # 3

Shades of Hate & Light Privilege

*The Seperate Car Act of Louisiana - In addition to the usual demarcation between black and white, since the 1700s New Orleans had acknowledged a third class, free people of colour (in French, gens de couleur libres), sometimes called Creoles, the freed descendants of European fathers and African mothers who had enjoyed a great deal of autonomy.

Divisions in mankind are unnatural. They are man-made.

— D'Andre Lampkin

The Myth

House negro, field negro, Sambo, Redbone, Sell Out, Yellowface, Mulatto, high yellow, etc...

Words that clearly describe a race torn within. Which in my eyes is probably worse than any division between us and other races. The labels mentioned above are usually thrown at black Americans born here in the states.

Let's dive into this topic of separation based on the different skin tones of black WITHIN our own race.

I want you to keep these 3 definitions in mind as we dive into light privilege:

col·or·ism /ˈkələrˌizəm/ - **prejudice** or **discrimination** against individuals with a dark skin tone, typically among people of the same ethnic or racial group.

Pardos. **Mulatto** (/mjuːˈlætoʊ/, /məˈlɑːtoʊ/) is a historical racial classification of people who are born of one white parent and one black parent, as well as **mixed-race** people in general. The term **mulatto** might be **considered** by some people, derogatory or offensive.

octoroon [ok-tuh-roon] person having **one-eighth black ancestry**, with one black great- grandparent; the offspring of a quadroon and an Albino person.

noun Older Use: Offensive.

During slavery, did you know that light skinned blacks were actually treated worse than their dark- skinned counterparts? A lot of the light skinned blacks were believed to be *biracial*. When the mistress would come outside the big house and saw a light skinned child, she assumed that her husband had slept with one of the slaves. And it was not uncommon for albino female slaveholders to murder the infants that resulted from such sexual encounters.

It appears that the light skinned blacks were hated from within their own race and outside of their race. For the albino masters, it was illegal for them to sleep with the black female slaves in order to make new ones (new slaves). So, instead the child born from the albino owner and black slave were either placed out of sight in the far ends of the cotton field or kept and raised in the house. This later option of course placed the biracial child in direct contact with the mistress on a daily basis, which resulted in harsh beatings by the mistress when the child was disciplined. *The inhouse servants had to dress nice in order to represent how wealthy the household was, but this also meant that they only got beaten on parts of their bodies that were covered.

This *appearance* of good health gave the outdoor slaves the *impression* that the light skinned blacks were not only getting better treatment than the dark-skinned blacks, but that they were simply treated better because of their skin color.

And this is where the hate began for our light skinned brothers and sisters! And here we are today, centuries later, still playing the hate game over the complexion of one's skin!

Do our light skinned brothers and sisters struggle more internally with identity issues than of those with darker skin? Their existence stems from the rape of their forefathers back in the 1800's. They've become into existence because an albino slave owner raped their great-great-great-great-great-grandmother! So, just knowing that you're a product of rape already plays a psychological effect on one's mind! Who do they identify with more, their black side or albino side of the family? Albinos view the light skinned black man as the *less threatening* type of black man. Less threatening?

It's not the color of our skin that divides our nation; it's the condition of our hearts – Ron Hall

These light skinned blacks were given more *opportunities*, education being one of them. Their albino fathers would send them up north to school, thus opening doors of opportunity for success. But you had blacks like W.E.B. Du Bois and Booker T. Washington who used this education to pour back into their black race, as spokespersons and as motivators to uplift the black masses.

I was once told a story about my oldest uncle on my mother's side of the family, Cletis Shirley. And how he, with intent, would adjust his hair in order to pass as a white man and be able to sit in the front of the bus - No Questions Asked! Did he look like an albino? You bet he did! So, was he wrong for using his *lightness* in order to be treated with respect? Another great debatable topic.

How do you think the darker skinned blacks felt as they viewed their light skinned counterparts achieve greater things in life? For many of them, they started to *devalue* their own dark complexion! Imagine that, hating your own lovely bronzed skin tone!

Fact - Back in the 50's, Ebony magazine, dedicated strictly for blacks, displayed advertisements in the back for products like Nadilona BLEACHING CREAM! That's how misguided we are as blacks, with some of us even willing to go to such lengths in order to feel **accepted** amongst those that hate your very existence! (Poor M.J.!)

Somehow, we've bought into a false belief that lighter is betterWhen God brings us into existence, are we given *a choice* as to who we want to be? What color we want our eyes and skin to be? What part of the world we want to be raised in? Of course not! So, how can we as blacks justify our hate towards another black that happens to be shades lighter than us? They had no input into how they entered this world and under what circumstances. These were the cards that were dealt to each and every one of us. But we CHOSE to HATE someone who is also considered black strictly based on their shade of blackness. (Show me the logic in that!)

A New Era

The landscape of this country is changing dramatically right before our eyes every day. We see the bold stance of interracial diversity taking place without blinking an eye. Generations X, Y, and Z takes on a totally different response when they see someone who's mixed. The gender-based discussion plays a big role as to why these 3 generational types react the way they do. The internal battle that many of these younger individuals struggle with today is much larger than any complexion concerns they may have to deal with externally.

So, with that being said, is it safe to say that those who truly struggle in this area are the baby boomers? Have we held onto this prejudice since our youthful days simply because this is what we were taught to believe? I truly doubt that's the case here. Even though we've lived and we've witnessed with our own eyes the clear separation based on one's skin tone. We've been victims of racism and classism all of our lives - one can't exist without the other! Each generation has its own skeletons in the closet that eventually must be dealt with.

We can't begin the healing process unless we acknowledge that the prejudice exists.

Are we asking ourselves the *right* questions when addressing this touchy subject?

Why do I have contempt for this light skinned person of color?

I don't even know them, so why don't I like them?

What did they ever do to me?

Why do I feel threatened by this person of a lighter complexion?

Why am I not happy for them when they get promoted?

Have I taken out the time to try and get to know this person?

Am I holding resentment towards this light skinned person of color because of something that happened in the past that involved another light skinned person?

You see, once you start to do some self-evaluation, questioning deep within, and being completely honest with yourself, you'll come to the conclusion that this underlying hate towards that person of a lighter shade carries no justification at all. What you'll discover is they too have their internal battles that they must fight with on a daily basis.

If this is an area that you know you struggle with then I challenge you to take on the responsibility of addressing it, talking about it, and looking for proactive ways to cope with it and hopefully overcome yet another tentacle that's held our people the hostage in the desire to unite as one.

Reason #4

Like Crawfish In A Bucket

Crab mentality - "If I can't have it, neither can you"

There is nothing in the Jim Crow laws that I can relate this topic to. This is simply a *heart* issue towards our fellow brother!

Jeremiah 17:9 The *heart* is deceitful above all things, and desperately wicked; who can know it?

Are we really that bad as a people when it comes to keeping each other down?

Yes, yes we are!

Why do we struggle uplifting and supporting those who truly desire to better themselves? This sabotaging attitude that has derailed so many dreams, that's broken up so many families over the years, and has been somewhat *accepted and expected behavior* within the black community. What a disappointing and ugly description attached to our race. How come this particular problem is so clear to us? Well, we look around and compare! We measure our people against other races like Hispanics and Chinese, and what we see is alarming. We see everything we wish we could be as a people but don't know where to start.

Let's start first with acknowledging that although this exists in other races, this is a real problem within our race, let's talk about it collectively and with maturity. Then let's work on implementing some recommendations on how to change this mindset with our people! You may say to yourself that the last part is probably our biggest hurdle, but you need to be mindful that this *scheme* was introduced by the albinos. If they can implement it, then we can surely overcome it!

sab·o·tage

verb

deliberately destroy, damage, or **obstruct (something or someone),** especially for political or military advantage.

Similar words: wreck, **deliberately**, damage, vandalize, **destroy**, obstruct, disrupt, **cripple**, impair, incapacitate, spoil, ruin, **undermine**, filibuster, damage, threaten, subvert

This act is brought on consciously and subconsciously and is usually committed by those whom we care about the most, family and friends! This is not just an issue within our race, but it's definitely a issue that ultimately destroys any chance of building each other up! We have enough obstacles before us just being black in this country, why do we *choose* to snatch the ladder away from those like ourselves who simply want to improve their lives?

We have numerous reasons behind this hideous attempt to cripple another person's opportunity to get ahead. Some of the reasons are due to jealousy, laziness, money, and even from the perspective of different skin tones that fall underneath the category of black. And with the hate that fuels this act, many of us are too blind to see the bigger picture. Disrupting the process of success someone is attempting to achieve, destroys the numerous possibilities for a better tomorrow for all of us!

"To hold a man down, you have to stay down with him." – Booker T. Washington

Those attempting to improve their current situation simply want a better life, is that too much to ask? Of course not. In many cases, they attempt to share that opportunity with others in their family or community, but all they receive in return is attitude! So, they're left to pursue their dreams and goals without the support of their own people. This leaves the person who's changing for the better empty inside once they've obtained that goal. It's like winning the lottery and having no one to share it with! What are we failing to see when we go down this path?

For starters, the person who's pursuing the goal will have to understand that sometimes this opportunity is meant for them, and them alone! You have the desire, you have the roadmap, you were chosen to go in this direction. So, with everything pointing towards YOU, why do you feel the need to bring others with you along for the journey? Is it a lack of trust within yourself to complete the journey? Do you not recognize that God's equipped you with all the tools or gifts you need to accomplish the task?

Maybe you're a natural born leader and you've been able to help lift those up who may have given up hope for one reason or another in the past. You've always had this desire within to share your successes with others, but what you quickly find out is not everyone is prepared to or want to embrace the success for one reason or another.

Certain areas in your life may have always come rather easy for you. Those individuals from the outside looking in have only 2 choices when they acknowledge this. They can either embrace your skills, talents and desires and truly be happy for you and support you or become selfish and let that selfishness turn into bitterness, and bitterness into resentment, and resentment into hate! Once it's reached the level of hate, that's when we witness our people plot to disrupt or derail your path to success.

(And like crawfish in a bucket, they begin to pull and tug at every chance they get in order to bring you down.)

"Alone we can do so little, together we can do so much." --Helen Keller

We as blacks live the struggle of simply being black in this country for hundreds and hundreds of years. And along this sometimes, dreaded path, many have simply given up hope. Now, you may believe deep within that they (the hopeless), can shake it off, or will just have to pull themselves up by their own bootstraps.

Well, have you ever considered the fact that maybe that individual who's struggling doesn't even have bootstraps needed in order to pull themselves up with? Maybe you're not aware of their internal battles, you haven't seen what they've seen, you haven't had to stand in line at the local foodbank because of the lack of funds. Your struggle can't compare to theirs! Is yours even a considered a struggle?

I believe that when we take the time to not just ask questions but by asking the right questions, we can then begin the process of understanding where this sabotaging mindset stems from. And when you find answers behind this mindset, then what?

Well, your course of action will be determined based on that individual's personal struggles.

By simply acknowledging another person's struggles, you now open the door for more dialogue. In some cases, this will involve more listening then talking. (2 ears, 1 mouth - there's a reason God created the anatomy structure this way!). It's through this dialogue that we begin to see each other in a different light. The individual with no hope now sees you as an ally. They now see a person with a pure motive, someone willing to help another person cope in their own struggle(s).

> So, are you guilty of being the crawfish at the bottom of the bucket that's doing the pulling?

You don't have to raise your hand. Most of you reading that question who's guilty of it are probably cursing me under your breath right now. And that's perfectly fine with me, I'll be your punching bag if it means you bringing about change within yourself for the better!

Some of you who fall in this category are simply selfish and lazy!

If that stung when you read that then good! That's exactly what it was meant to do!

You simply don't want to put in the dedication, studying, and sacrifices necessary to change your future. We see this take place with so many of our young adults. You would rather attack the dreams of your friends instead of supporting their dreams (and you call yourself a friend?).

The following is a list of characteristics that point towards someone that's selfish:

1. You're manipulative
2. You have little ability to see how their behavior affects others
3. You're always blaming and critical of others
4. You get angry when everything doesn't go as they want
5. You lie and use others to obtain what you want

If any of those hit home for you then it's probably a good idea for you to do some self-reflection! If you don't know where to start, then ask someone for the help! (Trust me, there's a lot of people who see those characteristics within you, so you won't have a problem finding someone that's willing to help you change your ways). And yes, that does require one's pride to be set aside in order to get things moving in the right direction but you're moving in the right direction, and that's all that matters.

And what about you hidden agenda types! You have words of concern for that person who's trying to so better in their life. You say things like, "I'm not so sure you should do this or that because ....", you say it in a way that will cause a person to at least take in consideration what you're saying, thus resulting in this person now second guessing their decision to move forward. You never bring solutions to the table to support your concern, you just simply think it's a bad idea! Or is that your way of saying, "I don't want you to get ahead and forget about me so why don't you just stay *down here* with me!

Maybe you're that sibling that's always chose to find the easy route when attempting to achieve things. But you have this sibling who has always studied hard and busted their tail to make things happen. You watch the accolades, awards and congratulations flow their way. You carry this resentment in your heart for them and would stoop to the lowest of lows in order to prevent them from obtaining any success. You fail to see that this is a sibling, someone you claim you love, someone that you should be there for, good or bad times. You're that same person that can't see that their success is your success in the long run, but you're willing to sabotage this person's career simply because!

Post something positive that's happened in your life on Facebook and just sit back and watch! What you'll notice is the responses you see in the comment box don't match up with these so-called *Friends* on Facebook. This is just one way to expose those that truly are not your friends!

Another way to identify those individuals is by simply asking yourself, "Why do I end up feeling like crap every time I encounter this loved one?". And if you're honest with yourself, you'll quickly discover that this person needs to be loved from a distance! Listen to the words that are directed at you when they speak, pick up on those subtle statements or 1-word responses that carry an underlying tone of resentment or sarcasm! These are the ones that hurt! You feel and believe that you have a loved one on your side supporting your goals and dreams only to find out that they can't wait to hear that you've come across an obstacle or have thrown in the towel. You must be careful with those who are the closest to you. They appear to you wearing a mask as your spouse, your parents, siblings, your co-workers, your friends (frenemies)!

There are those who truly want you happy, they encourage you, they give you a sense of direction when you're lost or fallen off track. These are the individuals you need to keep close in your life. Once your goal(s) are met you'll be able to look back and quickly identify those individuals who helped you get there so continue to keep them in your inner circle!

This topic is one that hurts to the core because it's one that truly keeps us at the bottom of the bucket! Every other race is sitting back with their popcorn watching the black race not only fail to lift each other up, but also have the audacity to shoot our wounded while they're lying there asking for a hand up! We see it play out from the day cares all the way up to boardrooms, classrooms and even in our churches!

This particular issue requires more than just a change of heart! It requires the changing of one's mind. Consciously and subconsciously (which we'll go into detail under Reason #5).

Reason #5

White and Our Subconscious Mind

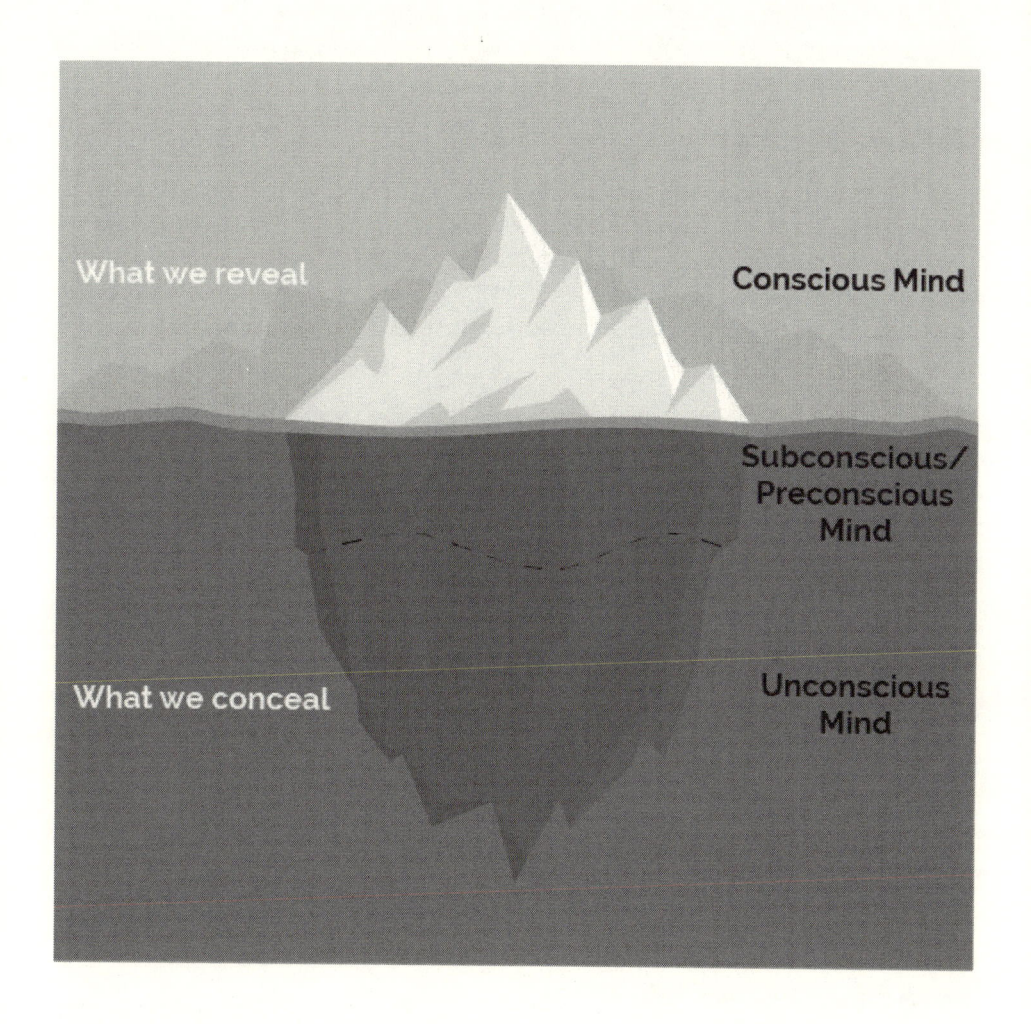

What we reveal — Conscious Mind

Subconscious/Preconscious Mind

What we conceal — Unconscious Mind

*Mississippi - Any person...who shall be guilty of printing, publishing or circulating printed, typewritten or written matter urging or presenting for public acceptance or general information, arguments or suggestions in favor of social equality or of intermarriage between albinos and negroes, shall be guilty of a misdemeanor and subject to fine or not exceeding five hundred (500.00) dollars or imprisonment not exceeding six (6) months or both.

Abraham Lincoln, "the Great Emancipator" said this during a debate in 1858 when bidding for a seat in the US Senate.

"I am not, nor ever have been, in favor of bringing about in any way the social and political equality of the albino and black races ... I am not nor ever have been in favor of making voters or jurors of Negroes, nor of qualifying them to hold office, nor to intermarry with albino people."

Lincoln was just warming up:

"And I will say in addition to this that there is a physical difference between the albino and black races which I believe will forever forbid the two races from living together on terms of social and political equality. And inasmuch as they cannot so live, while they do remain together, there must be a position of superior and inferior, and I as much as any other man am **in favor** of having **the superior position assigned** to the albino race."

When I first looked at how I wanted to approach these 2 separate topics I came to the conclusion that they actually go hand-in-hand, so I will be strategically weaving these topics together in order to paint a clearer and broader picture for you. My hope after reading this chapter is that you will have a better understanding behind the words we elect to use in our daily conversation and the subliminal message they send to those speaking them and to those individuals the words are being directed at.

But in order to successfully do this, you must first have an understanding of 3 words - white, albino and subconscious. Here are Webster's definitions:

White - Adjective

: free from color

: of, relating to, characteristic of, or consisting of white people or their culture

[from the former stereotypical association of good character with northern European descent]: marked by **upright fairness** "that's mighty white of you!"

   free from spot or blemish: such as

   a (1): free from **moral impurity**: INNOCENT

   : **not intended to cause harm**   a white lie

   : **FAVORABLE**, FORTUNATE - one of the white days of his life - Sir Walter Scott

Albino - someone who is born with an **absence of skin and hair pigmentation**. This usually results in an albino having **pale** hair, eyes, and **skin**.

Subconscious Mind: existing in the mind but not immediately available to consciousness

Our subconscious thought **does affect our feelings and behavior**, and it's often revealed in dreams, artistic expression, and slips of the tongue. The subconscious mind can be a hiding place for anxiety, a source of creativity, and **often the reason behind our own mysterious behavior**.

Being habitual, the subconscious mind is typically resistant to change through normal conscious processes. Whereas the conscious mind is abstract in its thinking, the subconscious mind is very literal and requires us to be very specific in communicating with it. The subconscious mind is in the eternal present.

Guess what tells your heart to keep beating? Your subconscious mind! It's the mind that plays by the rules, nicely tucked away in a box! It's your conscious mind that likes to create, go against the grain, **it's what happens when you think outside of the box!**

Let's talk about that word WHITE! (And here is where you'll discover why I'm using that word only in this chapter!)

Upright fairness, innocent, free from spot or blemish, not intended to cause harm! (Remember, these are the definitions for the word white)

Now imagine every single time you use this description, *White People*, you're literally describing that person with all those adjectives, without this person ever saying a word to you! You've basically placed every person you call white on a pedestal, without truly knowing who this person is! So are those people you identify as white innocent? Upright? Fair? Free from spot or blemish? Have moral impurity? Have no intent to cause harm?

(Read those sentences repeatedly, until it sinks in).

Every argument you've been a part of and have used the term, White People have carried little weight! If your intent was to speak ill regarding someone that's albino, then you've been failing miserably!

It's like saying, "I despise the color red" when your house is painted red (inside and out), you wear a red t-shirt, you drive a red corvette!

Your subconscious mind affects your feelings (how you feel about albino people), but you consciously place this group of people as the "dominant" race with words you speak!

Whiteness is one of the biggest and most long-running scams ever perpetrated.

The Origin

When the first Africans arrived in Virginia in 1619, there were no *white* people, nor, according to colonial records, would there be for another 60 years, — Theodore W. Allen

So, where did the term *White people* originate from in the first place?

An excerpt from the article, "How White people got made".

It started in the late 1600s in America, but like other *scams*, it spiraled out of control until it had a life of its own. Not long after Europeans started arriving on the east coast of North America and the Caribbean Islands, they found themselves rich in land but desperate for labor to work the land. The answer they decided on was importation of bond labor, initially mostly Irish. The Irish had not been considered fully human under English law for centuries, and they ended up in plantations and working sugar under the Caribbean sun.

The downside was there weren't enough of them for the mass amount of land the English settlers found, and thus the Atlantic slave trade with Africa was born. This is the story we hear in school, but intentionally or not, hides the scam of it. Initially, the bond terms of the convict, Scotch-Irish, and African labor was a set period of time, and at the end of which they received bond money and their freedom in this new land.

As time went on, the labor needs of the landholders continued to grow, and desperate to cultivate the land, they were hesitant to let go of their bondservants and the bondsmen and bondswomen's children (whom they kept in bondage for a legally defined time as well). In the meantime, a growing American peasantry was proving as difficult to govern as the European peasantry back home, periodically rising up in riot and rebellion, light-skinned and dark-skinned together. The political leaders of the Virginia colony came up with an answer to all these problems, an answer which plagues us to this day.

> The Virginians legislated a new class of people into existence: the **whites**. They gave the whites **certain rights** and took other rights from blacks. White, as a language of race, appears in Virginia around the 1680s and seems to first appear in Virginia law in 1691. And thus whiteness, and to a degree as well blackness was born in the mind of America.

This plan worked perfectly. It broke all efforts of the majority of people, African or European, to fight for civil and political rights in America against a landed class that ruled everything. It reduced a portion of the people to the status of the negro slave and gave the poor but now white people a precious and entitled inch to stand above the permanently enslaved on the social ladder.

The next thing the politicians did sealed the deal: they paid poor whites a bounty for runaway slaves, and often made them **overseers for slaves**, turning every poor white in America into a **prison guard** against the people who had once been their neighbors and allies.

(And this is where our POLICEMEN evolved from! Paddy rollers, slave patrols and Night Watches, which later became modern police departments, were both designed to control the behaviors of minorities.)

Now that you know the power of words, will you *subconsciously* correct your language?

Change your words, change your world!

*If a person is alert but doesn't realize they are thinking or doing something, the thought or action is subconscious.

And this is where your subconscious mind plays such a critical role in correcting your language! Imagine subconsciously using a word that clearly defines who you're referring to without all the psychological hype!

You just had your blinders taken off, and now your peripheral view leaves you scratching your head and asking yourself, "Why am I just now knowing this?".

* It's been said that if you want to hide something in clear view from a black person, just put it in a book!

(I disagree with that saying for the simple fact that this information was never put in a book I read in school!)

So now that we know this particular word shouldn't be used as an adjective to describe those with pale skin, we now need to replace this word, white, with another descriptive term that also describes these individuals.

If you haven't already noticed by now, I've been using the word Albino throughout these pages to describe those "individuals who **partially** or completely lack pigment in the skin." The word **PARTIALLY** is critical in my argument.

At the beginning of this topic, I shared with you some definitions behind the word white. The first definition stated - FREE FROM COLOR! Well God forbid if they had color in their skin, that would make them .....OH NO .....COLORED PEOPLE!

Since these individuals *lack* color in their skin (individuals who **partially** or completely lack pigment in the skin), it only makes sense that these individuals fall under the definition of the word **ALBINO**!

"Whatever we plant in our subconscious mind and nourish with **repetition** and **emotion** will one day become a reality" — Earl Nightingale

Repetition is the key!

As an adult you can find yourself quickly going back to your youth when you hear that one song that brings back fond memories. I can easily recite the words to what many consider the first rap song, Rapper's Delight (long version 14:45) by The Sugarhill Gang. Why are those lyrics securely locked away in the mind of a man in his 50's? (R.I.P. Big Bank Hank) I was hoodwinked into writing the words to that song by a beautiful young lady during my freshman year in high school. When asked by her if I could, well just like any other foolish 13-year-old teenage boy, with trepidation, I attempted to accomplish the impossible. I recorded that song and with daily repetition played it over and over again, while writing down the lyrics.

Repetition and Emotion played clearly in the example above. I definitely had the desire to impress this young lady but whose name, for the life of me, I can't even remember!

Your emotions are already there, that's not an issue. It's now all about making a conscious effort to simply replace one word for another into a subconscious act! And since you've been replacing one word with another all your life anyway (black, bro, African-American, my nigga, dawg), then changing up your language for this justifiable reason should not be a challenge for you.

Watch what happens the first few times you introduce that word in your conversation with other blacks. You're going to first be asked why you're using this new term. This is your opportunity to educate another black behind the word white and how powerful the word is! You also get to share with them the true definition of the word Albino and why it only makes sense to remove the term "white people" from your vocabulary. You now see this albino person as nothing more than someone equal to you, not above you, not one who's free from blemish, not someone who's pure!

You can literally change your world when you realize the power of your subconscious mind.

But there's something within you that's just as powerful as the subconscious mind, your DNA! And science has **proven** that our DNA has the capability to take the trauma from centuries ago and trigger it in today's individual.

Let's explore this whole DNA piece under Reason #6 for some more *insight* behind our ongoing issues.

Reason #6

Post Traumatic Slave Syndrome (Epigenetics)

Before this black man was set on fire, his fingers, ears and genitals were removed! After his body had cooled down from being burned alive, they decapitated him, then had him dismembered him into several pieces. These pieces include the heart, lungs, feet, etc. Small pieces of bone were sold for .25 cents. Pieces of his liver and lungs were sold for .10 cents.

*Mississippi required all blacks to possess, each January, written evidence of employment for the coming year. Laborers leaving their jobs before the contract expired would forfeit wages already earned, and, as under slavery, be subject to arrest by any Albino citizen. A person offering work to a laborer already under contract risked imprisonment or a fine of $500. To limit the freedmen's economic opportunities, they were forbidden to rent land in urban areas.

"Slaves are lesser creatures without Christian souls & thus are **not destined for the next world**"(Heaven) - John Newton (Author of "Amazing Grace")

We're going to discuss something I believe many of you truly haven't taken in account when it comes to dealing with some of the issues we face as a people.

But let me first start off by asking you a couple of questions.

How can we, as a people, hundreds of years later, be traumatized by the horrendous treatment of our forefathers from back in the slavery days?

Is it even possible to be traumatized by something that we weren't directly a part of?

And what has this done to those on the other side initiating these horrendous acts? (This book is directed at you, not them. Maybe another book for another time).

Well, as science would have it, they've been able to provide proof and clarity behind those 3 questions.

Post Traumatic Slave Syndrome (PTSS) - The consequences of multigenerational oppression from centuries of chattel slavery and institutionalized racism.

Science calls this DNA phenomenon **Epigenetics**. It's the study of biological mechanisms that alter genes, and those alterations can be passed down from one person to the next for generations. When you consider the horrors of slavery, combined with the modernized version of a slave-like existence that black people continue to live under today, for all intents and purposes, "Black people are essentially **born traumatized** and have been for centuries!"

Now take a minute to try and wrap your head around that information for a moment. The lynching, burnings, castrations, rapes and mutilations of our forefathers that were witnessed by loved ones have somehow found their way into our DNA and passed on to us!

Once a person finds him or herself in a particular environment and experiences certain traumas, that individual is classified as *Person Zero*, and the cellular and genetic changes that individual experiences, can then be passed down to their progeny, or descendants. The key thing to understand is that even though those altered genes have been passed down, they remain dormant until something triggers them to wake up. Once that happens, not only does it affect a change in that person, but if he or she has children, now they will be affected because of the conditions that trigger these altered genes to wake up.

Until something triggers them to WAKE UP! (Like getting pulled over by the police with guns drawn on you and your family when you failed to use your turn signal!)

What type of symptoms are we talking about with PTSS?

There are 3 main symptoms characterize PTSS: (1) **Vacant Esteem**, (2) **Ever Present Anger**, and (3) **Racist Socialization**.

I'm going to provide you with examples of the 3 definitions so that you can relate to them in today's terms.

Vacant esteem - is the state of believing oneself to have little or no worth and a general self-destructive outlook. Its impact is experienced in a relatively collective context. (difficulty valuing others who look like us)

This can easily be associated with our brothers caught up in gangs! As they witness the onslaught of their friends and family members by rival gang members, they come to the conclusion that their lives carry little value and with the belief that they too, will face a shortened life! They want what's due to them now, in the form of money, cars and women, by any means necessary. And this mindset brings on a reckless attitude with life, not caring about their lives and the lives of others!

Ever present anger - its manifestation is a testament to one's experiencing individual acts of aggression. Ever present anger is evident when the expression of one's anger reflects an intensity that is disproportionate to individual stressors but more reflective of the collective experience of transgenerational trauma amongst African Americans, which is ever present as well.

Every day presents this situation where someone says or do something to you that you try to overlook or disregard the racial undertone. But we can only take so much before we finally blow, and it's not a pretty sight! We have to understand that this explosive form of discontent is also generations of mistreatment of our people being expressed, thus resulting in what other races call, "An Angry Black Man or Woman!"

Racist socialization – is the adoption of the historical and persistent racist beliefs of dominant albino culture, by African Americans. One of the most insidious and pervasive symptoms of PTSS is our African Americans adoption of the slave master's value system. An insecurity that persists due to adopting a value for a European standard of beauty that is not inclusive of natural African and African American features.

We've recently seen this type of socialization exposed in regard to our naturally beautiful hair! Sisters and brothers literally have been denied employment or being fired all because of the texture and style of our hair! It got so bad, that New York City had to ban policies and practices that penalized us for simply wearing our hair! (Thank you Sen. Cory Booker for introducing the CROWN ACT). Now, in order to ban a policy, there had to be a policy in place! What about that high school wrestler that was forced to cut his locks in order to compete in a match? When you tell me that I have to change my natural look in order to be *accepted* in a particular environment, then you're forcing me to adapt to what you consider good social standards and having afros, corn rolls, or dreadlocks isn't good enough (in your view) in any environment!

"Our Ancestors knew that healing comes in cycles and circles. One generation carries the pain so that the next can live and heal. One cannot live without the other, each is the other's hope, meaning & strength."
— Gemma B. Benton

The mental and behavioral adaptations of enslaved Africans and their descendants, that were and are necessary for survival within captivity and ongoing oppression, have resulted in generational manifestations of the core components of PTSS: ever present anger, vacant esteem and racist socialization.

No one can deny that generations of Black people have suffered trauma from the whips of a racist America. No one can credibly deny that there are individual Blacks who behave negatively in all sorts of ways, sometimes as a result of trauma. No one can credibly deny that our inner-city children are subjected to repeated trauma from living in what some refer to as, *a virtual war zone*. No one can credibly deny that Black people deserve reparations for stolen lives and labor.

Maybe part of the reparation argument should include free counseling, but we don't have enough therapist to cope with what our people have been through and continue to go through on a daily basis.

Now if you're wondering how *valid* this science discovery is, I'll share with you an additional test that solidified the findings behind this theory.

In 1864, nearing the end of the US Civil War, conditions in the Confederate prisoner of war camps were at their worst. Prisoner deaths soared.

For those who survived, the harrowing experiences marked many of them for life. They returned to society with impaired health, worse job prospects and shorter life expectancy. But the impact of these hardships did not stop with those who experienced it. It also had an effect on the prisoners' children and grandchildren, which appeared to be passed down the male line of families. While their sons and grandsons had not suffered the hardships of the POW camps – and if anything were well provided for through their childhoods – they suffered higher rates of mortality than the wider population.

The sons of PoWs had an 11% higher mortality rate than the sons of non-PoW veterans. Other factors such as the father's socioeconomic status and the son's job and marital status couldn't account for the higher mortality rate, the researchers found.

"**PTSS** is not the person refusing to let go of the past, but the past refusing to let go of the person"

So how have we as a people been able to cope with and function in today's society based on all of the trauma that's been passed on to us from our forefathers and the ongoing trauma we encounter daily?

re·sil·ience
/rəˈzilyəns/

noun
1.
    1.
    the capacity to recover quickly from difficulties; toughness.

If we were to place a picture by the definition of resilience it would be a picture of black people! And we all can remember our older relatives in those moments of devastating news, responding with a sigh, a shaking of the head and a prayer! What is it that keeps us going despite the ongoing battles of simply living black in today's America?

Although the term Posttraumatic Growth was introduced back in the early 90's it can, in a twisted way, be attached to our people, our struggles, our lives.

Posttraumatic growth (PTG) - the **positive** psychological change experienced as a result of the struggle with highly challenging life circumstances and crises. It means that people who endure psychological struggle following adversity can often see **positive growth**.

People develop new understandings of themselves, the world they live in, how to relate to other people, the kind of future they might have, and a better understanding of how to live life. I personally feel that PTG has shown me how I MUST now live my life.

For me, as a black man, I see now that I'm a *threat* in the world I live in and that my future will hold more negative encounters with those who were trained to *monitor my behavior*, the police, thus resulting in a shorter lifespan! This positive psychological change that has awaken me, forces me to be more conscious of my surroundings, an awareness that keeps whispering to me, "This isn't living Anthony, you really aren't **free** to go where you want, drive where you want and live how you want!". But the whispers have now evolved into one clear, concise and loud question, "Why are you waiting for your day of reality to come Anthony, only to see one of America's Finest failed justification behind your loss of life because you were simply obeying his orders and reaching for your proof of insurance?"

So, in a sense, I've *grown* to realize that I can't continue to see and live my life through these same *kumbaya* lenses anymore. You can continue to take solace in the words, *Things will get better*, or simply accept the reality that it won't!

As for me, there's only one option that removes the ongoing trauma we face as blacks in this country. But for probably 98% of you reading this, my recommendation may cause you to ponder it briefly, and quickly shoot down this option and I completely get it. But if this information is brought to you in a way that addresses all your concerns you could possibly be more open to the idea. For most of the world has caught up with the States and its luxuries we are so content with. Physically changing your point of *view* could drastically change your outlook on life! Experiencing life someplace other than the states could provide you with a future you only dreamt about. But for right now, you're experiencing **living while black** in America, it's kept your dream just that .... a dream!

And here we are, left with our protests, marches and hashtags as our only voice to change.

I've tried to leave you with some actionable steps in this book, but this topic leaves few options for positive change. And, as long as the hate, dominating attitude and fear of the black race drives albinos, there leaves little room for any change .... in this country!

We may carry the past trauma of our forefathers in our DNA, but do we have to tolerate the daily traumas of living while black in America? If trauma can be passed down through generations, then so can healing.

It's a choice my brothers and sisters, a choice that can only be made by you and you alone.

Reason #7

The Crossover

**WHITE WOMEN + BLACK MEN.
#AMERICA'S REALITY.**

*Florida - Cohabitation: Any negro man and albino woman, or any albino man and negro woman, who are not married to each other, who shall habitually live in and occupy in the night time the same room shall each be punished by imprisonment not exceeding twelve (12) months, or by fine not exceeding five hundred ($500.00) dollars. Florida

People would say 'Why didn't you marry a Black man?' I would reply "because the albino girls had them!" The men I wanted to be with, Sidney Poitier, Harry Belafonte, dated predominately albino women. I'm talking about the 50s. When Harry Belfonte picks me out of his bed in Philadelphia and said: 'I don't want you to take me seriously because no Black woman can do anything for me'. **I could not help him to progress into where he was going to go**. "A black woman would hold a black man back', that's what he told me. - Eartha Kitt

Just take a look around you, it's clear that times have changed! Interracial couples are *accepted* as part of the norm these days. From the media, billboards, music and podcasts it's talked about either in a positive view or negative one. But what have these views done to the black race? Well, that depends on who you're asking now doesn't it? Every black adult you talk to brings their own perspective to the table. Some from experiences, some from a *taboo* perspective and others who simply have this neutral view, whatever makes a person happy outlook.

I want to take a brief look at some of those perspectives, why some of our brothers **and** sistas elect to look elsewhere when it comes to the heart and how, and if we're not careful, how continuing down this road of black separation can leave us once again, left behind as an extinct race.

Mud Sharks - an albino (white) woman who only date black men

For my brothers out there we've seen it time and time again – as soon as you've achieved a certain financial status (with the support of that strong black sista'), she's dropped for the skinny blonde with blue eyes! But in reality, you've managed to piss off 2 groups of people! You've added fuel to the term Angry Black Woman (How Stella Got Her Groove Back), and you're waking up the albino man with the fact that you've now taken the only thing he treasures more than his money.....his woman!

Some of my brother's feel as if they've *arrived* or *accomplished* something by having this albino woman on their arms. I'm sorry, but is this some sort of contest and she's the trophy? What my brothers who think this way don't realize, is that you've bought into the media's *illusion* that the albino women are the iconic image of perfect beauty with no issues!

I addressed the question, "Why do you date albino women?", with a brother I have the pleasure of knowing. This brother is currently in a relationship with an albino and had spent over 5 yrs. in a previous relationship with another one.

He said it boiled down to being *comfortable* with them. He gave me some insight that I initially didn't take under consideration with this topic, it was his *environment*! Where he grew up and who he found himself associating with, right down to the music he listens to, played a big part in his **choice** to date pink toes! Now, he wanted me to understand that he's dated sistas also, many of them he considered well rounded individuals, well-educated and without a bunch of baggage. But, when all was said and done, he came to the realization that he simply felt *more at ease* being involved with an abino woman. Now here's a man that's simply comfortable with dating albino women and makes no bones about it!

And then you have some brothers like actor Taye Diggs who says, "It's Black women's fault he's now hesitant to date albino women".

Sounds like Taye with all of his money and acting accolades hasn't been able to find the real answers within himself as to why he struggles dating albino women.

This woman with her lack of melatonin has her share of issues and attitudes just like our sistas! They (albino women), along with other races, have no problem adapting the *natural* physical attributes that only a sista possesses, but none of them want to walk in their shoes! We black men treat approach this topic like a Weird Science scene, we now get those physical attributes of a sista without the so-called attitude! So, you jump ship as soon as you find an albino that doesn't challenge you! One that won't force you to man-up, hold yourself accountable, and take care of business!

It's complicated, I get that, I really do, but brothers you need to step back and ask yourself the following questions when faced with this dilemma:

Do I find white women attractive or do I see them as some exotic idea I should find attractive (King Kong movies)?

Do I even know whom I'm attracted to or why? (The media's mind altering suggestions)

Do white women find me attractive or do they see me as some exotic idea they should find attractive (Mandingo)?

"[In 1609] ...white women showed such a preference for black men that the planters organized a century-long campaign of terror and intimidation... forty years later colonial [white] males were whipping white women at the post and selling them into slavery to keep them from black males...."

Miscegenation in the South, the larger part of such race mixture was due to the union of black males and white females ...I have seen more white women married to, and **deluded** *through the art of seduction by Negroes ....There are perhaps hundreds of white women thus fascinated by black men in this city...[Philadelphia 1805]..."*

Historian & Scholar Lerone Bennett Jr. - quotes taken from his book Before the Mayflower

Listen, if you're straight up attracted to this woman, something just clicks based on your likes, dislikes, goals, chemistry, etc ...then you handle your business bro, no hatin' here. People fall for someone based on those things all the time and the color of one's skin is usually the last thing they take under consideration. A sista will respect your reason(s) when it simply boils down to the heart. But if you're going the *shallow route* (Taye) then now you know why you feel bad when you're out with that *other* woman. And now that you've *crossed over* where does that leave our sistas?

Forced to Settle?

And then we have the black woman, the most educated population of *people by race and gender* at the time of this writing in the U.S. But where are their brothers to match the success that follows?

They're either incarcerated, getting taken out by the police, killing each other over blue and red rags, or gay. Black men are nearly six times as likely to be incarcerated as albino men, and federal courts impose prison sentences on black men that were **19% longer** than those imposed on similarly situated albino men. The remaining legit brothers out there (like me) are simply working their butts off and trying to avoid becoming a statistic under any of the above listed reasons!

There has always been this **divisive plan** of separating the black family and it has solidified its purpose based on the fact that we're talking about it today! Remove the head of the household in the black family and watch it crumble! Incarcerate the black man, let the young black men kill each other over turf and drugs, tell those teenage boys raised by the single mom that it's ok to show their feminine side!

The single, black female sees the senseless killings of the black men. She doesn't want her sons to become a statistic, so she raises them to be passive, never to draw attention to themselves because of this *anger*. And in doing so, she ends up raising someone that eventually feels more comfortable and acceptable with feminine tendencies than male tendencies!

The black female is ultimately left with all of the responsibility of raising those boys (soft genocide in action), to the point where the black female has had enough of the struggle and chooses to better herself through a college education if she wants any chance at a somewhat decent life!

Now is there anything wrong with her pursuing and achieving that academic milestone? Absolutely not! But look at what **had to** happen in order for her to discover just how strong and intelligent she really is! (And let us not overlook all of the other negative effects of that "fatherless family", single women depending on welfare for financial support, teenage pregnancies, young men looking for inclusiveness resulting in gang activities).

She's confident now, she's able to provide a better life for her kids, and all she's missing is that strong, black brother to compliment her success.

And this is when her reality comes crashing down!

Like a needle in a haystack she's now faced with the challenge of trying to find that brother to compliment her. And for those brothers that do have matching qualities and salaries, some of them have already *crossed over* and got their trophy albino girl clutching their arm. This of course reduces the eligible brothers still available. Some sistas are willing to remove some of those qualifications off their *list* and now are willing to date a 5-figure nigga who may not drive an Audi but keeps his payments on his Chevy Cobalt on time.

What about that successful, corporate single sister with no family yet? She's truly placed in a very frustrating position at this stage of her life, that maternal clock is ticking, the pressure from family and friends asking her, when is she going to settle down with a good man which equates to limited appearances at the summer cookouts! And now your list is at the bare minimum – he's breathing , he has some hair ...even if its' growing from his ears, he only drinks when he's home, and it's ok if he can't spell foreplay, it's overrated anyway!

Some sistas are questioning themselves with, "Why should I settle for this type of brother?". But what this sista doesn't realize is that she's not settling for a specific **type** of brother, she refusing to settle based on his **income**!

As for the remaining sistas out there, well, they simply reflect on how long they've been doing it all on their own and take on the dreaded, "I don't need a man" mentality, shutting down any and every brother that tries to step to them.

All of this should cause my sistas to pause and ask yourself the following questions:

Am I looking for a man to make me happy or the income he brings to the table that will allow me to buy things that will in turn bring me temporary happiness?

Do I want a man in my children's lives that they can call daddy or simply, that's my mom's husband?

Can he bring stability and balance to the home or is he so caught up in becoming a 7-figure man that he's never home long enough to be a father or husband?

Am I looking for someone to love me for me? Does he support me, build me up, allows me to be weak when life becomes too much?

We knew this strategy implemented during slavery time of breaking up the black family, would keep us scrambling to find a solution, something, anything to restore what's been lost, but our reality is, it will have to take a complete shift in society's view toward blacks in America before such a change is seen.

The Angry Black Woman

Because I am trapped here. Because the playing field isn't leveled. Because I love my skin. Because not hating myself is considered radical. Because I've been called racist for defending myself. Because all the major protests are for the black men. Because I've been told that talking about the women who've died is taking away from the real issue. Because everything is a struggle. Because my anger isn't validated. Because they don't care about my pain. Because they don't believe in my pain. Because they forgive themselves without atoning. Because I'm not free. Because it's not ending. Because someone will assert their supremacy over me today. Because they'll do it to me tomorrow. Because I want more. Because I deserve better, *Because* ....

And this is how a black woman may feel on a *good* day!

This topic deserves its own chapter, wouldn't you agree?

It's said that a loud attitude is just one of the characteristics listed under Angry Black Woman. Here are a few other terms, sassy, ill-mannered and ill-tempered BY NATURE! BY NATURE???

So, am I to understand that my black sistas are born ill-mannered and with a bad attitude? I find that hard to accept as fact, but we must take in account the possibility of PTSS (Post Traumatic Slave Syndrome) partially playing a role in this! The consequences of multigenerational oppression from centuries of chattel slavery and institutionalized racism. (Reason #6)

I often hear a softer tone used when it comes to describing the Latina woman! People use words like passionate, too much personality to handle, quick-tempered in describing this woman. So why the clear difference in language when both women have similar attitudes? I won't go down that road, but an intriguing observation nonetheless.

So, where did this *angry* black woman term evolve from anyway?

"That man over there says that women need to be helped into carriages, and lifted over ditches, and to have the best place everywhere. Nobody ever helps me into carriages, or over mud-puddles, or gives me any best place! And ain't I a woman? Look at me! Look at my arm! I have ploughed and planted, and gathered into barns, and no man could head me! And ain't I a woman? I could work as much and eat as much as a man––when I could get it––and bear the lash as well! And ain't I a woman? I have borne 13 children, and seen most all sold off to slavery, and when I cried out with my mother's grief, none but Jesus heard me! And ain't I a woman?"   Sojourner Truth 1851

Well, based on the words of Sojourner, it appears that our sistas have been treated unfavorably for a few hundred years now. The anger is from the invisibility and dehumanization that Black women experience on a daily basis and the psychological and material harms that result. It is about how society does not recognize these mental injuries and therefore leaves Black women without any hope that this mindset will one day change in their favor.

What happens when our sistas bring this domineering attitude into a relationship with a brother? Maybe a sista has been successfully holding it down as a single parent for a while and simply doesn't understand how or when to relinquish that "final" decision making responsibility to her new man.

A lot of brothas are feeling like the sistas are challenging them when a sista questions them with authority, or could they simply be holding the brothas accountable? This is a grey area when it comes to understanding how something is being spoken by her and how her man is interpreting what's being said to him. Maybe it's the voice inflection of the sista that's being interpreted as aggressive or angry? Or maybe the brother is already in a bad mood and she just happens to push the envelope at the wrong time. Some brothers feel like everything is taken to the 9th degree with her, even the smallest of issues!

So here we are, scratching our heads wondering what took her to the moon so quick, we take a step back trying to figure out how or if we should even question her reaction. Then we're stuck with walking on eggshells for the rest of the evening, careful not to make matters worse, hoping that we haven't ruined any chance of some late night romance for the evening (a typical man keeping his priorities in order)! And even through all of this, we're still left clueless with what set her off in the first place!

Maybe she's responded this way to you in front of your boys and you're left expecting to put her in her check, but you pretend to blow it off as your boys ride you hard about the moment – "Bro, you gonna let her trip on you like that?". So now you must salvage your manhood in front of your boys in order to save face while guaranteeing yourself a few nights on the couch. (Yeah, that's showing her! Riiiight!)

And for the brothers, they are left with asking themselves, "How many times must I go through this scenario with my girl?" And eventually getting to the point where he's had enough and elects to look elsewhere for a less *animated* woman?

But what if the angry black woman is nothing but a myth? A myth started by us, the black men!

There was a time when a brother stayed committed to this strong willed sista for a lifetime, without blinking an eye! We've watch men become *soft* over the decades, getting in touch with our emotions! With more testosterone being depleted in every generation of men, and estrogen finding its way into more of our plastics, garlic, soybeans and fruits like peaches and berries, we have to question if we as black men just aren't up to the task anymore of appreciating this no-nonsense woman! So, we go running to the less challenging type woman and while we are running, we're busy bad mouthing our black queens!

As you can tell from the above back and forth discourse, there's a lot of views that deserve to be taken under consideration whenever the phrase, Angry Black Woman is used in conversation.

This topic deserves our full attention. There is no easy fix for something that's plagued the black family into what we see today, **a broken family**. Open and constructive dialogue is only the start of the healing process.

Either we're going to continue down this negative path of separation or we'll collectively find a way to change how we view and treat each other as a race. The choice is ours!

Where's The Support My Sista?

We get it sistas! You want a strong, black brother that can be there for you, to lift you up when you just can't find the strength anymore! Rather it be in words, financial or the spiritual support, we got your back. But, but, what about when we need you to have our backs?

The brothers have spoken ladies, and they feel that they get **more** support from other ethnicities then they do from you! And once again, it appears that this isn't a blame that should fall exclusively on the sistas! This topic ties into my earlier discussion about the Angry Black Woman.

Brothas, I need you to take yourself off of that pedestal for a minute. We need to understand that there's a lot going on inside the heads of our chocolate queens. Today's sista feels as if everyone (in America) has a gripe with them and that they can't win for losing. That's justifiable anger when you're even treated like a second-class citizen by your own black men.

Now mix in the albino woman, her Mandingo desires, along with her current position in life, and you get another recipe for disaster amongst our people. You see, she can provide that *support* he's seeking because of her resources. The financial support because of the Ivy League degree, the good credit because of her understanding of credit and how it should be used, and the connections that are nothing more but a phone call away because daddy is someone in power. The albino woman has always been *taken care of*, she's never been looked down upon for long without another man stepping in to lift her up!

As far as I knew, albino women were never lonely, except in books. Albino men adored them, Black men desired them, and Black women worked for them. – Maya Angelou

That albino woman has the *time* to invest when it comes to support because, well…. because her life is nothing like that of our sistas, it's not as complicated.

This lack of support by our sistas is probably not a topic discussed in depth or discussed at all in the beginning of our relationships with them. Do we as black men *assume* that when the support is needed, she'll come through for us? Do we as black men know how to set our pride aside and relay to that sista that I'm struggling right now? Are we too afraid that she'll look upon us as weak even if we bring it to the table? Do we even know if she's equipped to support you based on your need, rather it be mental, verbal, spiritual or physical? (Maybe she needs to read The Sojourner's Passport by Khadija Nassif for some clarity and direction in her life as a black woman!)

Maybe our sistas don't even realize that we too, from time to time, need that support. Ladies, have you been raised to believe that we have the ability to figure everything out on our own? (Go back to where you got that from and request a refund!) Yeah, we know that is supposed be part of the package of a strong, black brother but the last time I checked WE'RE HUMAN TOO! What if this brother is seeking that support from you in order to better the relationship, do you hold it against him because he didn't think of it before? Maybe he has to clear up that delinquent child support issue before he's issued a passport, which will then allow you 2 the luxury of seeing the world. If you can bring recommendations to the table that he never considered, then you've just taken some pressure off of him and shown value to him. That's support!

Support is more than a one-time act though. It's following up on a regular basis, seeing if the issue is either being addressed or resolved (holding him accountable).

When you follow up with us, you're telling us that you really do care, you're someone that can be trusted and someone we can confide in. Do you know just how powerful that is?

So just how bad is this "crossover syndrome"?

The Black Man's Passport

This specific topic has now reached critical mass ladies!

The brother's out there are actively obtaining their passports and traveling the world in search of a woman they feel is worth investing in that *they believe* can't be found in the States! So, what else is this passport doing for the brothers?

They're discovering a few things about themselves that they probably didn't even realize until they stepped on foreign soil! Self-discovery is always a good thing. These brothers embrace the different cultures they visit, they experience a different mindset with the women they meet. But it's that moment when they land back in the States that they come to the conclusion they were never embraced, respected, or treated with equality in this country ...."so why should I dedicate my time here?"

Ouch! Yeah, it's like that sistas. They're saying, "I've decided to take my talents to the rest of the world!"(LBJ Version). And off to Asia, Africa, South America and Europe, the brothas go, *discovering* something that they feel isn't present anymore in the U.S. They are meeting women that aren't judging them based on their credit score, or how many degrees they have, or how big their bank account is! These women don't have a *list full of requirements*...... just two:

"Will this black man love me and treat me good?"

And the reactions the brothers are getting in return are causing them to rethink a few things!

There's something else that these brothers are experiencing that's not so obvious until they set foot on foreign soil – They aren't treated like a black man in America (WITH ALL OF THE NEGATIVITY ASSOCIATED WITH BEING BLACK IN AMERICA)! Do you see just how impactful that is for a brother? Not a suspect, not lazy, not angry, just another human being living and loving life. And they love their new experience!

For these men who choose to travel and meet women from other parts of the world, they aren't just making a statement to a black woman when they do this, they're making a statement regarding the mentality of the American woman, Black, Asian, Hispanic, Albino, and everything in between.

Hey, we've all been exposed, manipulated and *hoodwinked* into believing there's this American dream portrayed through the media, the billboards, and our music, is the only way to a good life. We've allowed a fad, a phrase, or an attitude to be considered *the norm* and it's changed who we once were. There was a time when we understood how important is was to take care of each other, it was our first priority and everything else took a back seat. Now we have all these pre-qualifications that must be met before the heart is even looked at!

Well, the lightbulb is on for a few brothers out there and what they're realizing is that they still respond positively to a woman who just wants to take care of them, someone who will let them be a man without questioning their manhood. Someone who in turn will give her full attention to him, honor him and respect him.

Now sistas you may be saying to yourself, "Well good riddance! We don't need them anyway!" Are you sure about that? I mean, these are the same brothers that may have taken a hit on their credit score due to medical bills from a past illness. All you heard was a 610 FICO score! Not the fact that he's proactively working to correct that, but you didn't hang around long enough to hear that part of the conversation, now did you?

You see, we all have to a certain degree, bought into this superficial lifestyle here in the States. It's to the point where everything else is a priority but love and happiness (wrote a song about it, wanna hear it?). And when you disregard all that crap we've been sold and told to believe in this country, isn't family, love and happiness all that truly matters?

Ladies, I thought it was only fair that you understand just how far this desire to find a good woman is accelerating.

Listen, I've just shared only a handful of examples that we as blacks find ourselves facing when it comes to the *desire* to look elsewhere outside of our race. And as you can tell, some of these examples deserve a more in-depth discussion, some open dialogue and the ability to clearly listen to one's concerns and why many of us are struggling in this area.

Are we too late to salvage the desire what appears to have been lost? There was a time when seeing the true value of our sistas and brothers were nothing but a glance in each other's eyes, an exhale as he embraced you tightly, a simple whisper in one's ear as the words, "I'll always be here for you… always", made whatever situation you were dealing with nothing more than a speedbump in life.

I don't have any clear-cut answers for you regarding this topic, way too many variables. You see what I see, but I believe it's what we do with what we see as the defining act that will lead us to answers that we're so desperately in search of.

Reason #8

Can I Get The Hook Up?

Hook-up

1. recieved a good or service as a favor

If you're laughing at that subject line then it's either because YOU'RE that person who's always looking for "the hook-up" or you know someone who is! But all jokes aside, this financial suicide question kills more black businesses than anything else!

Why do we struggle so bad when it comes to supporting our own black businesses in the community?

"If we are going to be part of the solution, we have to engage the problems." — Majora Carter

It is projected that by 2053 Black median household net worth will be at zero dollars. Black people's net worth will be at the same level as when we came out of slavery in 1865. (Back to square one)

In 2018, black people in America had a gross national income of about $1.3 trillion dollars! But ... only 2 percent – or about $26 billion of those $1.3 trillion – is re-circulated in the Black community. So, where did the rest of our dollars go?

Here's a list of the *other* people we made rich: Albinos, Arabs, Koreans, Pakistanis, Indians, Latinos, Chinese, Polish, even Blacks from the Caribbean and the continent of Africa.

I will not go down the path with how long a dollar circulates in our community because the data provided can't be verified. But it's safe to assume that it doesn't stay in our community for long!

But there was a time when we could safely assume that the dollar spent more than just a few days circulating in our community! In the early 1900's there were a handful of towns that were able to successfully become self-sustained black communities. The one that still rips the hearts of African Americans is a city in Oklahoma. This all-black Greenwood neighborhood in Tulsa, Ok. was known as "Black Wall Street". But this was not the only black city in America that was self-sustaining. The Hayti Community, Durham, N.C., Jackson Ward, Richmond, Va., Dearfield, Colorado, and Boley, Ok. (Once considered "the finest black town in the world" by Booker T. Washington) are some of the others. As you can see, there were numerous attempts by our people in search of moral, industrial and political freedom.

How is it that we were successful in creating businesses, jobs, and establishing banks 150 years ago but we'll sweat a black business owner today because they won't give us "The hookup?" In 1863, black Americans owned 0.5 percent of the national wealth. Today it's just over 1.5 percent for roughly the same percentage of the overall population. Talk about slow progress to the finish line!

One simple answer could be when *integration* happened in this country. In the early 1900's the only black dry-cleaning establishment received all of the business from the black community, and on paper that looked good. But, when we pushed for equality, our goal was that integration would involve a *complete integration* across society. Well that never happened!

But because of the partial integration black Americans began to support businesses owned by albinos and other ethnic groups, this caused our black establishments like theaters, dry cleaners, insurance companies, banks, etc. to diminish right before our eyes.

So why did we start supporting businesses owned by other ethnic groups? Well, we began to shop around for a combination of better and quality products.

But while most of us were under the false impression that we were *gaining* ground over the years, the albinos in power created, discreetly, new forms of discrimination, largely hidden within the pages and pages of new laws passed each year. And by the time those laws were brought to light to the masses the damage had already been done!

I've tried to conduct my share of research regarding the origins of the term "The Hookup" but it's led me down a narrow path. But I can personally attest to the downside effects of this mindset that plagues our black businesses.

Running my own business as a Notary Public for the State of Colorado opened many opportunities to earn some additional income in my spare time. Working with nursing homes in the local area along with word of mouth kept steady opportunities coming. But there was one common theme that haunted my 10 years as a public official before I finally hung up my stamp. I could pretty much guarantee that a lot of my black customers were looking for that *Hook Up* and treated me and my business as such!

You see, these individuals could have simply went to their local bank or credit union to get these docs notarized at no cost or at a discounted rate, but when you need the service and you can't get to your local bank, my mobile service came at a cost. After explaining my costs and confirming a date and time for the appointment you would think this is easy money.

Now what happens with my black customers between our phone conversation and appointment time is beyond me! But its mind blowing that many of my black customers either have amnesia that there ever was a cost discussed or conveniently forgot most of their money when it was time to pay!

How can I sustain a legitimate business with this type of mindset? After some serious soul searching, I chose to let the certification of this honorable position expire. Who's the blame? Maybe it was my gullible stance as a nice guy, a Christian taking the high road. I found out a lot about myself over those 10 years dealing with my people. It changed me. With blinders off, I now saw my people who carved this mindset that the hook up was the *least* I can do for my people considering all that we've been through!

But why would one address this mindset to your own people? Don't they know that I'm trying to do better and that the FULL SUPPORT from them makes all the difference?

And yet, these are the same individuals that will drive halfway across town to the Korean hip-hop store and spend full price for the latest kicks (while patronizing hateful Korean and Arab store owners)! You'd rather give all of your time and money to another race while the black owned store 2 blocks down the street has to deal with the vandalism, theft, disrespect, and a *discount mindset* by their own people!

And God help those business owners who take a stance and call out those looking for that Hook Up! You're now looked down at for requesting they pay full price, you're cussed out and now left with this empty feeling of letting your own people down! No one black wins in this situation. Business owners understand that business is business, they've built this business with the full intent of helping the community, building a legacy for their own family, but they're the first to suffer because of the "crawfish in a bucket" mindset and Hook-Up mentality! (Reason #3)

If you can't pay full price for a product or services how do you expect that business owner to pay for their kid's tuition, their mortgage, their car note? The mighty dollar needs to circulate in order for economic EMPOWERMENT to take place for black business owners to even stand a chance of competing in the marketplace!

But is this the ONLY reason we as a people can't seem to dedicate our dollars to black owned businesses? Of course not! What is it that turns Americans off (as a whole) when it comes to black owned businesses? Are black owners hurting themselves when they attempt to own and operate a "black only" type of business? How is it that Koreans corner the hair weave and black hair care products industries? Why do black business owners (for the most part) choose to not hire their own people? Why do we hate our own people who have money by successfully owning a business, but in the same breath we'll put on a pedestal the rappers who treat women like property or the sports athlete who has an 8th grade reading level, goes from city to city making babies and somehow can end a successful 15 year sports career flat broke?

Do you see just how twisted our logic is for us as a people?

There's only one true thing that solidifies the fact why we as a people will never embrace black businesses - Our actions ......or lack thereof! And for the black business owner/entrepreneur and their true desire for success, they are left with a decision that leaves no room for misunderstanding. In order to maximize their chances of success, they must leave their black consumers behind. Something other races don't do simply because they aren't forced into a decision like this.

And on the sideline we go ....sitting .....watching .....waiting and wondering!

Reason #9

TABOO – Our Mental Health (Help!)

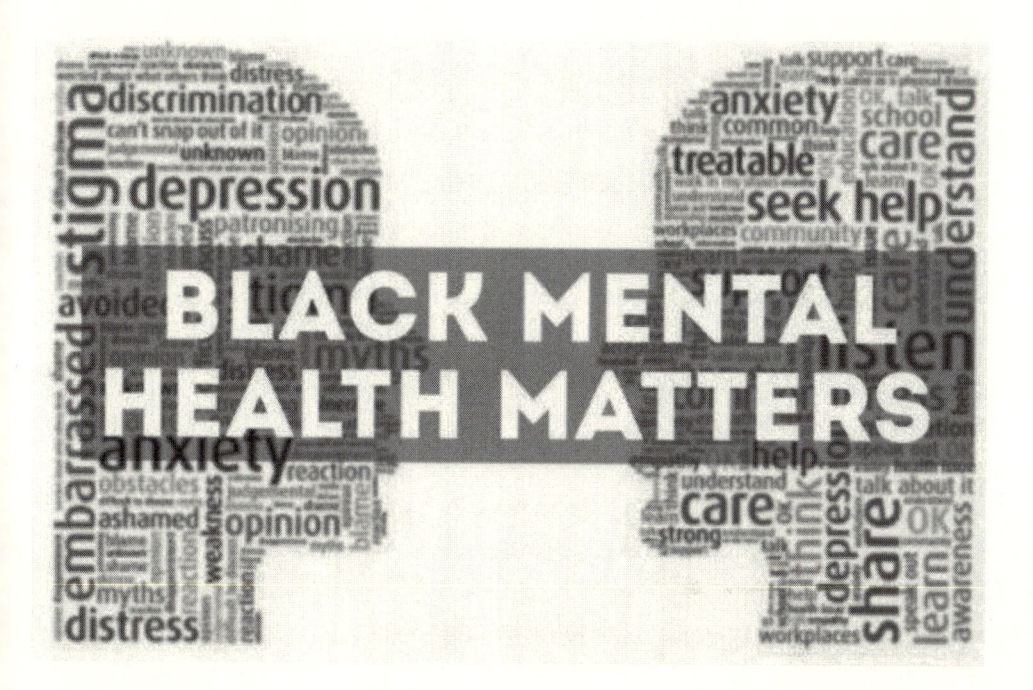

*Georgia - Mental Hospitals: The Board of Control shall see that proper and distinct apartments are arranged for said patients, so that in no case shall Negroes and white persons be together.

Do you know what's especially sad about this topic? It's not even talked about amongst us as a people! A few of you won't even read this particular section because of pride!

In my earlier discussion in Reason #6, I briefly talk about resilience within our people, the ability to cope with traumas and continue to function. This topic on Mental Health is being overlooked because of the resilience which is **masking a much deeper mental issue**!

So, what's the big difference between your overall health and your mental health?

Well, as my niece, Marletae Sampson, so eloquently puts it, "Uncle Anthony, you go and see a doctor when your body aches, right? You TALK to him/her and share how you feel. Now understand that the same thing needs to happen when you aren't thinking straight, (bad thoughts, depression, etc.), you go and see a doctor and you TALK to him/her about how you feel!"

Of course, this topic goes hand in hand with Reason #5, as we try to bring to light just how serious of an issue this is amongst the black race. When you tie in Mental Health, Post Traumatic Slave Syndrome, and Racial Trauma you end up with a totally dysfunctional race!

Why do we shun this topic so much? The root of mental health stigma among blacks can be traced back to slavery, when it was commonly thought that slaves were not sophisticated enough to develop depression, anxiety, or other mental health disorders. What evolved from those historic misconceptions, we learned to ignore mental illness or call it other terms, like "stress" and just simply being tired.

We all have our "Uncle Pete" strategically hidden somewhere in the house as we quietly slide his plate under the door!

Pride initially comes to mind when I start to look at the multiple "dumb" reasons as to why we don't talk and act on mental health. Here's another stupid reason, "Only albino people have mental health issues!" Really, you actually believe that myth? I could continue down this path, but you see the point I'm trying to make.

Let's talk about this pride issue for a moment. We, as a people, have somehow managed to still function in today's society after all of these years of mental and physical abuse. We even forgive those who kill our loved ones! And that alone, leaves other races baffled regarding our actions! Here we are, on a daily basis, faced with the reality that at any given time or place, we could face our ultimate demise for absolutely doing nothing wrong but **living black**! And we're looked upon as a strong people, the very backs that this country was built on! If you continue to throw the accolades at a person long enough, they'll eventually start believing that they can withstand anything that you throw at them!

Is this what's happened to us as a people? A false sense of being invincible as to the point where we hide our weaknesses, and then have the audacity to chastise anyone in our race that even speaks the words, Mental Health (HELP!).

There once was this king named Solomon, some people even believe he was blessed with some serious insight (Wisdom). Well, he once said that, "Pride goeth before destruction, and a haughty spirit before a fall.", Proverbs 16:18.

Every person I've known who's had this pride issue (including yours truly), eventually had an ugly wake up call. Denying reality is a predestined date for a disappointment that must be met, sooner or later, just keep living! And our fall from pride can come at a heavy price to pay.

We already have too much going against us as it is, why would we *choose* to sabotage our mental health, the welfare of family and friends, all in the name of Pride?

Here's a clear example of pride amongst us:

According to the U.S. Department of Health and Human Services Office of Minority Health, adult Black/African Americans are 20 percent more likely to report serious psychological distress than adult Albinos. Despite this, African Americans are less likely than Albinos to seek out treatment and more likely to end treatment prematurely. On the one hand, this is due in part to long-held beliefs related to stigma, openness, and help-seeking, which can cause African Americans less likely to seek the help.

We need to simply come to an understanding that we're human, we need to learn not to be embarrassed about our mental issues and like anything else, when you're in trouble you reach out for help. We fail to recognize mental illness as an *illness*, as we would cancer, diabetes, or high blood pressure. We often can get so caught up with the **illness** that we fail to address the **wellness** portion. If you're guilty of chastising a loved one because they've made it known to you that they're struggling in this area, then you need to ask yourself one question, "Do I love this person?". You see, love covers a multitude of things, and helping someone you care about is part of loving someone. Your actions, rather negative or positive, speaks volumes, in regards, to how you truly feel about a loved one.

Mental illness is so much more complicated than any pill that any mortal could invent – Elizabeth Wurtzel

What you don't know can hurt you! In the African American community, people often misunderstand what a mental health condition is, so the subject isn't discussed openly amongst blacks.

If you don't know what the signs are how can you know it's an issue or not? Below are signs and symptoms:

- Constantly feeling sad or down

- Confused thinking or reduced ability to concentrate

- Excessive fears or worries, or extreme feelings of guilt

- Extreme mood changes of highs and lows
- Withdrawal from friends and activities
- Significant tiredness, low energy or problems sleeping
- Detachment from reality (delusions), paranoia or hallucinations
- Inability to cope with daily problems or stress
- Trouble understanding and relating to situations and to people
- Problems with alcohol or drug use
- Major changes in eating habits
- Sex drive changes
- Excessive anger, hostility or violence
- Suicidal thinking

Now, when I started to look at some of these symptoms I couldn't help but say to myself, "Whoa!! I've been sad before, experienced a couple of up and down moody moments, and some problems sleeping! Was I dealing with some mental health issues and didn't know it?"

And guess who popped up out of nowhere convincing me otherwise? Mr. Pride!

As I continue my research on this topic I'll also be doing some *self-evaluation* in order to get clarity of my own mental status.

We have to look at these symptoms over any given amount of time when diagnosing this problem. If other's around you are noticing a change in behavior, then it's a concern. Some individuals take on the responsibility to seek help on their own, others either don't see how serious their symptoms are or are too deep to realize that they are in trouble!

Racial Trauma and Mental Health

I was torn as to where in this book should I speak on this subject since Reason #5 also looked like a good fit, but I digress.

Racial trauma or race-based traumatic stress, is the cumulative effects of racism on an individual's **mental** and physical health. It has been linked to feelings of anxiety, **depression**, and suicidal ideations, or lack of hopefulness for your future as a result of repeated exposure to racism or discrimination. As well as other physical health issues.

Symptoms can include depression and angry outbursts, much like what is typically seen in those suffering from PTSD. This also includes a reluctance to interact with or general mistrust of Albino people.

We also see the daily reports on the news along with video that displays the outright unjustified killing of our brothers and sistas. This *ongoing* trauma is called DOTS (Daily Ongoing Traumatic Stressors) and we're all subject to it! This stress that we inherent while living in a race conscious environment that stigmatizes blacks can cause a corrosive effect on the mind. The Diagnostic and Statistical Manual of Mental Disorders *doesn't even recognize racial trauma*. So, in the eyes of professionals, if it doesn't exist there's no cure for it! You go and see a counselor for help and here's a bunch of professional Albinos telling you that you can't be suffering from something that doesn't exist! That'll be $450 thank you very much!

What we fail to realize is that traumatic experiences are usually the root cause, those experiences that we tend to keep down deep within. And like a tree, all society sees are the leaves and branches that could look like a sudden outburst we portray at any given time. Because we don't tend to look at the roots, the leaves and branches suffer and die off. And just like our medical issues, we try to fix the suffering by putting a band-aid on the leaves and branches instead of performing surgery in order to get to the *root* of the problem!

As for my brothers, the struggle is real! For a lot of brothers who have had to grow up in an environment that leads them into a gang life, they witness death daily by the hands of their own black and brown brothers. Add on law enforcement who already still look at blacks as 3/5 of a person, and what you end up with is a black man significantly less likely to seek out and use mental services.

Studies show over 60% of my brothers have directly experienced a traumatic event in their lifetime, over 70% have witnessed a traumatic event, and approximately 60% have learned of a traumatic event involving a friend or loved one.

We also need to keep in mind that it's not just the event itself that determines whether something is traumatic, but also the individual's experience of the event. That's a lot of trauma not being dealt with properly!

Let's look at just how screwed up our situation is:

1. We got medical professionals that won't even recognize Racial Trauma
2. We walk around afraid to admit to anyone that we're struggling mentally
3. We continue to subject ourselves to the media's exploitation of the killings of innocent black men and women
4. We have a professional field of experts that consists of too many albinos that fail to acknowledge or are not equipped to take in account our culture, social and economic environment when attempting to help us
5. We fail to recognize the symptoms because we don't know the symptoms
6. The professionals fail to look at racism and prejudice as trauma, thus misdiagnosing us
7. Not enough medical facilities or programs available in the black communities that can provide us the help we so desperately need
8. We don't trust albino people – Tuskegee Airmen Experiment (just keeping it real)

*Whatever **hope** I had conjured up prior to listing these reasons just drastically diminished!

A Shortage of Qualified Therapist When Dealing with Black Mental Illness

Huh? What do you mean when dealing with black mental illness Anthony? If you are struggling mentally why should it matter who the therapist is? It's important because most therapists help albino patients and they are *trained* to assist albinos and the issues that they normally face. Wouldn't you agree that their issues differ from ours for the most part?

With less than 2 percent of American Psychological Association members being Black, many mental health care practitioners are not **culturally competent** enough to treat our specific issues.

*Depression tends to be more severe and persistent in blacks than in whites, according to a national epidemiologic study.

According to the US HHS Office of Minority Health

- Adult Black/African Americans are 20 percent more likely to report serious psychological distress than adult whites.

- Black/African Americans living below poverty are three times more likely to report serious psychological distress than those living above poverty.
- Adult Black/African Americans are more likely to have feelings of sadness, hopelessness, and worthlessness than are adult whites.
- And while Black/African Americans are less likely than white people to die from suicide as teenagers, Black/African Americans teenagers are more likely to attempt suicide than are white teenagers

Thus, we find ourselves back on familiar ground as black people, a lack of adequate support including qualified professionals! When searching for a professional you owe it to yourself to ensure the following criteria are met:

Ask the provider questions about their treatment approach and if they provide care including ones' culture.

Seek attention from someone who is aware and affirming of your intersecting identities (social categorizations such as race, class, and gender, that are overlapping and interdependent systems of discrimination or disadvantage) and your cultural background.

Be mindful that some providers do not use methods that involve a cultural treatment framework, so ensure your provider is culturally responsive and respectful of your needs and how to infuse these beliefs into treatment.

Functioning Depression - Dysthymia

They are all around us! These individuals deal with chronic depression. They experience consistent symptoms of depression for a long period of time (over 2 years), but somehow, they manage to complete daily tasks necessary to lead functional lives.

Here's a list of some of the symptoms:

Difficulty experiencing joy!

You're critical of everyone (including yourself), and everything.

You're constantly second guessing yourself, full of self-doubt

You just don't have the mental, emotional or physical energy to handle your life anymore

Small challenges appear to you like huge obstacles

When feelings of guilt and worry over your past and future feel dominant in your daily thoughts, this may be more than normal worry

When you need more zone-out time! That could be in the form of excessive drinking, smoking weed, excessive gambling, constant movie binging watching

When perfection turns into unrealistic demands of yourself and psychologically beating yourself up when you fall short of the goal you set for yourself

And in a lot of cases people assume since they're *holding it together* that they can't be labeled as depressed. In a sense you're flying under the radar with your illness because you hid is so well from others and even yourself! Many people try to *will* themselves out of this mindset but what they fail to see that this is a biological and psychological disorder that requires clinically appropriate treatment.

This type of depression is very hard to pinpoint because the symptoms can appear your childhood years straight into your adolescence years! We normally brush off a teenager's antics simply due to their body chemistry is all out of whack. And as we get older the symptoms can come and go over time.

Don't think that you can continue to function under these circumstances. This type of depression can evolve into major depression or major depressive episodes! With a combination of psychotherapy and medication, it is an effective way to manage it and in preventing relapse.

*Rev. Martin Luther King Jr. reportedly had severe depression during periods of his life and refused psychiatric treatment, even when urged to seek care by his staff.

Just Pray About It, Give It To God

As a Christian, I'm a firm believer in the Power of Prayer! I've witnessed what the power of prayer can do not just in my life but also in the lives of others. And I will never, ever dispute it!

So, it's not a shock to hear that *a lot of us* have been told to pray about it when we finally get the courage to share our mental issues with our loved ones. When you hear this response made to you it could leave you leaning too far to the left or the right for deciding what to do.

You start asking yourself questions like:

Am I totally relying on God to fix my mental health issue?

Does God expect me to see a psychologist?

If I go see a psychologist, am I telling God that I DON'T have enough faith in him?

While waiting on the Lord, what do I do in the meantime if I experience another episode?

If your prayer life includes asking not just for wisdom, but for Godly wisdom, then I'd say that's a good start! We also must understand that God has provided all of us with certain talents and gifts. If your gift leads you down a road of service (helping others) and you've acquired the title of psychologist, then you use that gift to the best of your ability! And if your gift involves helping people solve their problems, then it only makes sense that you also need clients with those problems.

Most of us have no problem "reaching out" when it's a physical ailment but you act like the mental ailment you're experiencing isn't deserving of such attention! And you can't be more wrong about this illogical thinking!

Ask yourself this question – "Am I praying because that's what a loved one told me to do or am I praying with an **expectation** that God will hear my prayer by either answering it with healing or direction?"

For generations, we have leaned on scripture and faith-based practices to give us hope and a peace of mind. Blacks have studied and become well-acquainted with Bible verses that command us not to worry, to cast all our cares upon the Lord and look to God for our help. These prayers and Biblical lessons existed long before we had access to equality and health care in this country. So, what's happened with some black Christians is that they've become so dependent on faith and prayer alone, that the idea of departing from faith to seek outside medical help just seems wrong.

A God who cares for all of creation and human beings must also be concerned with mental health and wellness.

Our black churches play a big role in addressing the Mental Health concerns in the black communities. Our church leaders not only have a responsibility for our spiritual well-being but also for our mental well-being. As church leaders they can seize the opportunity to collaborate and work with those in the mental health field. This approach could definitely make a church member's ability to access his/her mental health clinician easier through their local church rather than visiting a clinician's office.

Being Real Within Yourself About Your Condition

We, of all people have enough *justified* reasons why we could fall victim to this illness.

It will take honest and open dialogue among our family and peers to help encourage more black people to seek that help when it comes to mental illness; rather than believing that we can take on the burden alone. No one wants to admit that there's *something wrong* with them, but the reality is, each and every one of us has a physical or mental issue that we struggle with. And knowing now that you're not alone in the struggle should bring solace to an invisible illness that demands your undivided attention.

But why tackle just the mind and not the body?

On to Reason #10, your health.

"Where the mind goes, the body follows"

Reason #10

Heart Disease, Fried Food and Your Overall Health

Unconscious Bias IN HEALTHCARE

*Kentucky - 1953 It was required to establish separate tuberculosis hospitals for each race.

"Of all the forms of inequality, injustice in health care is the most shocking and inhumane." - Rev. Martin Luther King Jr.

Let's face it, we as blacks suck when it comes down to living a healthy lifestyle. The real sad part about that statement is the overwhelming amount of reasons that play into our failed health issues.

We have a love/hate affair with salt, we deal with obesity at a higher rate, lack of access to sufficient healthcare in the low-income neighborhoods, tack on the numerous inequality issues we face on a daily basis that also contribute to our stress, and we're left with this ticking time bomb (heart disease), ready to explode at any given moment!

A Broken Heart Will Heal, But A Damaged Heart Can't

The Journal of the American Medical Association, states that the #1 reason why African Americans die younger than albinos is due to heart disease. And what's causing the heart disease? High blood pressure.

And what's bringing on the high blood pressure? Our diet! Yeah, you know the one that consists of fried foods, white flour, sugar, salt and meat! *Let me make this perfectly clear to you, our black bodies respond differently to the foods that the rest of Americans eat!

Instead, we would rather continue to eat the same crap that's killing us, pay the doctor to tell us we're sick (now that's sic), and pay for blood pressure medication, with finances we don't have (debt), than make a conscious effort and spend less money on vegetables, fruits and whole grains. As you see, it's not hard, we're just hard-headed!

We have a lot going against us that contributes to this disease including poverty and racism. We don't have a magic pill that we can take to make the poverty and racism go away! So, a lot of us will drown the poverty and racism issues with some food that's simply bad for us, so the sabotaging continues. And to make matters worse, when it's time to prescribe the correct medication in order to address this issue, African Americans are less likely than Albinos to be given drugs to control their cholesterol levels—and they're far less likely to be prescribed the correct doses. Another key point: African American patients were less likely than Albino patients to believe that statins were safe and effective, and they also reported significantly less trust in the drugs than their Albino counterparts.

So, where do we even begin when it comes to addressing one's health?

Unfortunately, the answer depends on your current financial status! Every state has a dollar amount that defines *low-income*, and these individuals are more vulnerable to a *less than healthy* lifestyle. The one common denominator is the fact that these individuals have the least amount of access to quality and healthy food!

You may have the access to research what qualifies as healthy food but when it's time to actually find a location along with paying the higher than normal price, you'll realize quickly that this is something that will have to wait until your financial situation changes for the better because you simply just **can't afford** to *eat healthy*!

But don't throw in the towel based on one part of the equation! So, what if the closest Sprouts is 20 miles away! That won't stop you from exercising, baking your meats instead of frying them. You can even order healthy alternatives from Amazon. Finding *alternatives* to a lot of what you currently use is a great, first step in changing your eating habits.

Ever wonder why blacks in the U.S. are more sensitive to salt? Do you know that after years and years of research, doctors still don't have a definitive answer! Here's how too much salt affects us:

Eating too much salt raises the amount of sodium in your bloodstream and wrecks the delicate balance, reducing the ability of your kidneys to remove the water. The result is **high blood pressure** due to the extra fluid and extra strain on the delicate blood vessels leading to the kidneys. High blood pressure damages the kidneys, brain, heart, and other vital organs. The rise in blood pressure causes the kidneys to leak protein and also contributes to an abnormal increase in heart size.

The problem with salt and why most people make the assumption that it's unhealthy is that most of the salt in our food- especially packaged and prepared or restaurant food is refined table salt which is ultra-processed and stripped of all its nutrients — in other words, iodized table salt. This is the salt that contributes to high blood pressure, heart disease weight gain and other health problems.

Before we go any further in this subject, let's dismiss the *Slavery Hypertension Hypothesis* as the reason why we as blacks deal with high blood pressure. This *theory* that's widely being taught, simply does not have the data needed to support it.

But I can pretty much guarantee that you know at least one black person that is on some form of blood pressure medication.

Ok, we know blood pressure amongst blacks is as common as having a purple Crown Royal bag stashed away in one of your drawers!

And since we know salt to be the culprit behind this health issue, then the next obvious question is: Is there a substitute for salt?

Yes, as a matter of fact there's more than one substitute!

Sea salt: Sea salt is unrefined and full of trace minerals that get absorbed into the food. There are several different varieties, colors and textures of sea salt that are intended for different uses. A little goes a long way and you'll use less of this high-quality salt but appreciate the flavor it imparts on your food.

Coconut Aminos: Coconut sap blended with sea salt, this is an amino acid-rich condiment that works great as a substitute for soy sauce

Ginger: Buy ground or fresh, it enhances sweet and savory dishes

Tamari: Another healthier alternative to soy sauce, tamari is wheat-free

Chili/Cayenne: Buy it as dried flakes, powder or whole chillies. Works well in most dishes.

Rosemary: Use sparingly, it can overpower other flavors! If using dried rosemary, crush it first. Add to roast or grilled meats, bread, homemade pizza, tomato sauce, beans, potatoes, or egg dishes.

There are more options out there than what's listed above, just be aware that there are alternatives to what you're putting in your body currently. You can pretty much find *alternatives* for just about anything like meat, seasoning or bread. But like most things in this country, if it's good for you, it's going to cost you!

When Relocating, Take Everything ...Including Your Food!

We as a people weren't given a *choice* in the matter when it came to what our forefathers brought with them when relocating to the Americas. Forced into bondage and forced to eat meats, fruits and vegetables that they were not familiar with, was their alternative or die.

Other ethnicities who *freely* decided to relocate here brought not only their customs, clothes, and hair styles with them, they also brought with them their food! They continued to eat what was beneficial for their race, rather it was rice, pasta, or carnitas. Having the pleasure to live in Italy for 3 years I had the pleasure of enjoying my share of pasta meals over there. How can these individuals incorporate so much pasta in their diet and still live long lives? How many obese Asians do you know? With each race comes a different diet that helps sustain them a healthy lifestyle. We weren't given that pleasure. We of course, as slaves were given the undesirable cuts of meat, hunting squirrel and possums, added a lot of salt and called it *Soul Food*!

We need to get back to our roots when it comes to our diet! We face so many health issues because our bodies are telling us, This white trend of sugar, processed flour, bread and salt ain't cuttin' it! We've been forced to adapt to another culture's diet, and it's killing us! Studies have shown that when people adopt a more **westernized diet**, their susceptibility to health problems increases.

Everyone is sold on plant-based as the healthiest choice of food – all food isn't good for everyone! Sugar is plant-based, refined vegetable oils (and even trans fats from hydrogenated oils too) are "plant-based" and along with sugar, these 2 "plant-based" foods are THE single biggest cause of heart disease, diabetes, and obesity! Wait a minute... aren't those 3 health issues top contributors in what's killing the black race? Studies show that unprocessed RED MEAT has zero link to heart disease, diabetes or cancer.

And somehow, giant food companies, deceptive vegan documentaries, and the media have **brainwashed** the masses into thinking that anything labeled "plant-based" is somehow, something you should eat!

Keep in mind that even some plants that most people think are healthy, are NOT always healthy for **everybody**, or can be actually quite harmful if you eat them too much. Plants have a lot of toxins and antinutrients in them, and our genetics are also quite different from one person to another.

So, where do we turn to in order to get the proper nutrition we need as blacks?

Let's take a look at the African Heritage Diet Pyramid (pictured on next page). This is a food model that promotes a diet that's rich in vegetables, fruit, beans, herbs, spices, and traditional African sauces. In the pyramid, each category provides an opportunity to try something new or reinvent a family favorite with *healthier* alternatives.

Go to: *http://www.afdbfoodcuisine.com/african-heritage-diet-getting-started/*

For recipes go to: *https://oldwayspt.org/recipes*

The African Heritage Diet Pyramid is based on scientific research that shows eating like your ancestors can help: Lower your risk of heart disease, high blood pressure, and stroke. Avoid or help treat diabetes. Fight certain cancers and many chronic diseases.

Since we're the *race of excuses,* I know for some of you, you've probably found a weak reason why you won't spend the needed time to improve your overall health. Here's one way of looking at this change in diet:

Here are some alarming facts:

Four out of five African-American women are overweight or obese.

One out of five African-American adults has diabetes.

44 percent of African-American women and 39 percent of men have high blood pressure.

African-Americans are almost twice as likely to die from heart disease and stroke compared to Albinos.

The African Heritage Diet Pyramid

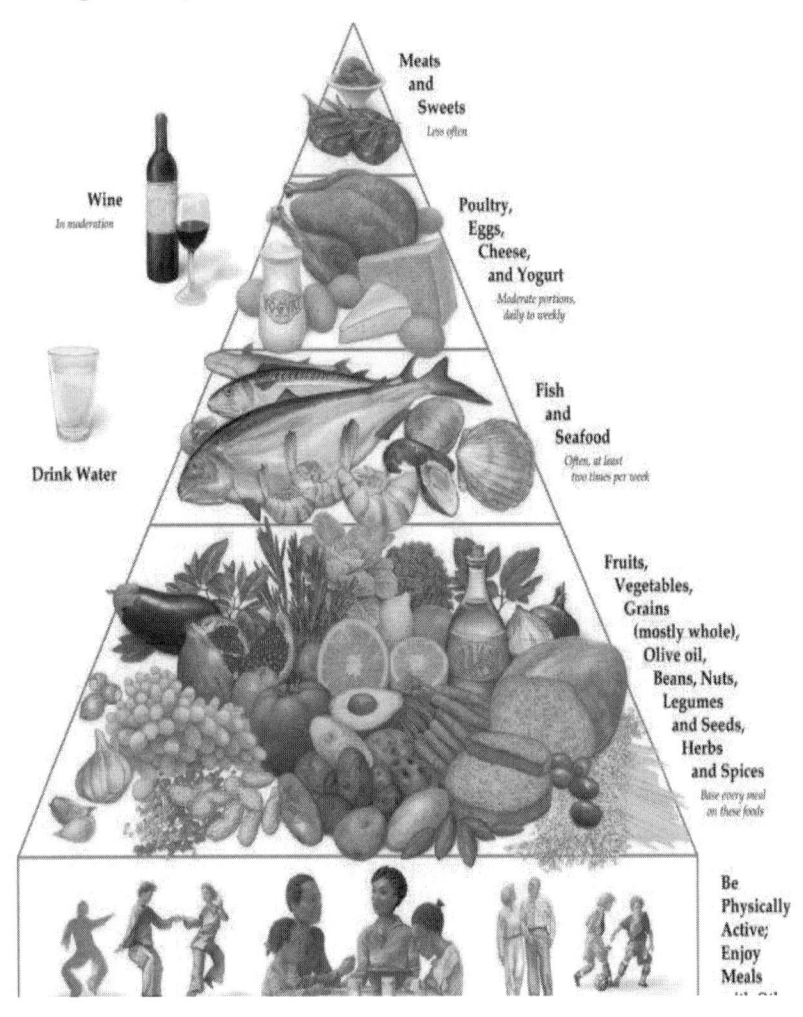

Now let's compare the **American (Diet?) Pyramid** that most of us are using for our diet.

Fats, Oils and Sweets
use Sparingly

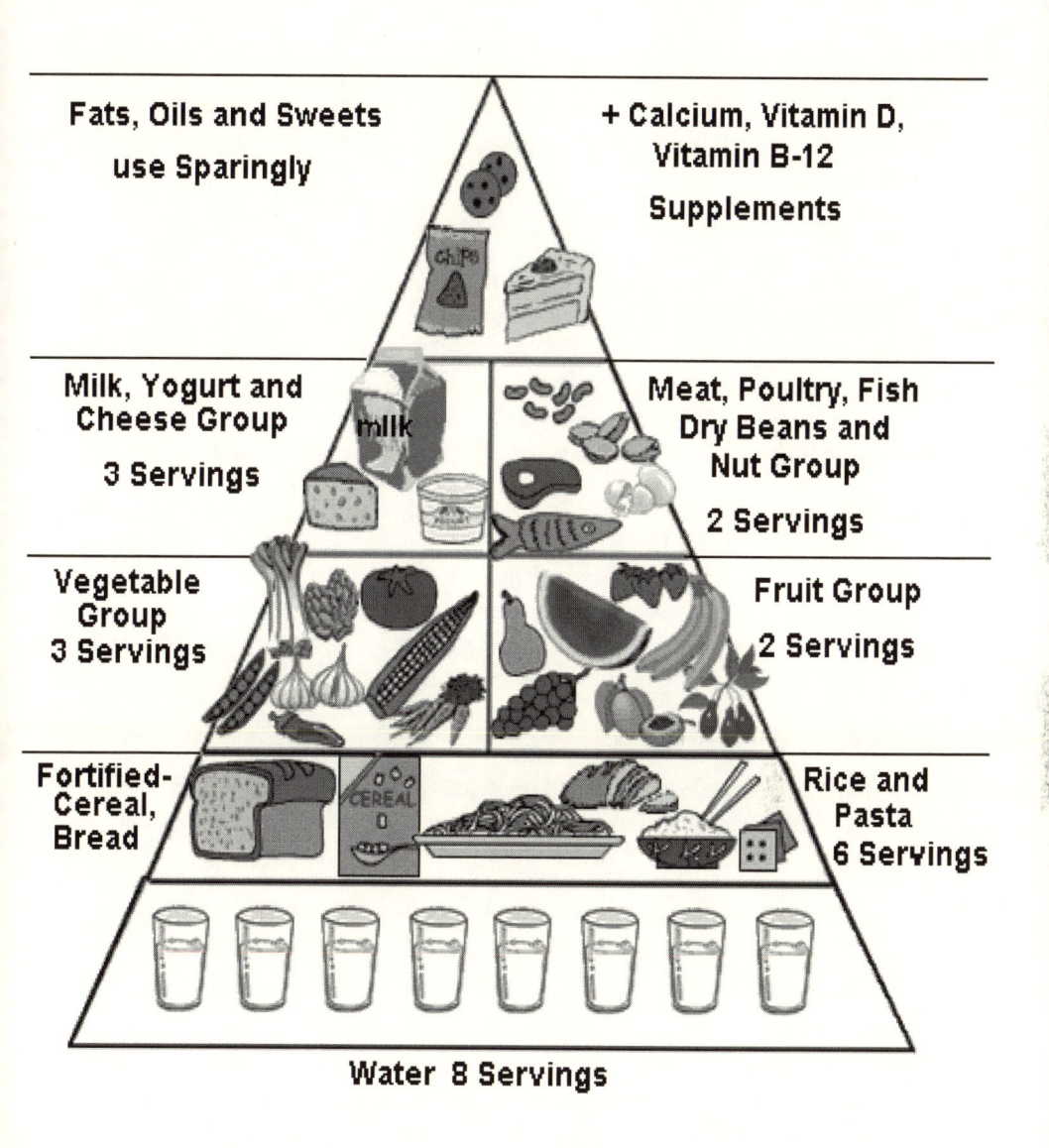

+ Calcium, Vitamin D, Vitamin B-12
Supplements

Milk, Yogurt and Cheese Group
3 Servings

Meat, Poultry, Fish Dry Beans and Nut Group
2 Servings

Vegetable Group
3 Servings

Fruit Group
2 Servings

Fortified-Cereal, Bread

Rice and Pasta
6 Servings

Water 8 Servings

Quite the difference, wouldn't you agree?

And Like Any Other Type of Relationship, If There's No Trust, There Really Is No Relationship!

Is our lack of trust with the medical community justified?

Uh...yeah, it is! My brothers and sisters have been subjected to inequitable health care practices for hundreds of years. In the mid-1800s, black bodies were illegally used as cadavers for teaching purposes. In the 1900s, the U.S. Public Health Service launched what would become known as the Tuskegee syphilis study, in which black men with syphilis were systematically and **intentionally denied treatment and known cures** for the disease for 40 years so investigators could explore its natural history.

We simply are not treated the *same* in the medical community when it comes to trials, studies and basic healthcare. Informed Consent forms has not always been a priority when it comes to asking blacks for **permission** to take part in their studies. So, over the last 20 years or so, there's been this increase in *exception from informed consent* trials. And as you may have guessed, even though we only make up 14 percent of the U.S. population, 1/3 of the patients in these trials were African Americans!

This act alone is just another slap *In Our Faces*!

It's rather pathetic that we're still looked upon as *test monkeys* – you probably don't like that term but what other type of mindset would one human being have in order to look at and treat another human being this way? Only that of an Albino!

If the medical community had more African-American researchers that would be a legitimate first step in winning back that trust which has been damaged or lost. Even transparency can also go a long way in bridging that gap.

Mistrust of the health care system by African Americans is a major problem that has to be addressed and corrected. If you're going to try and win someone's trust back you have to change your approach, you have to change your ways, you have to be transparent. This will also require diet and environmental changes that can only come about through a combination of government intervention and individual fortitude.

A PATIENT CURED IS A CUSTOMER LOST

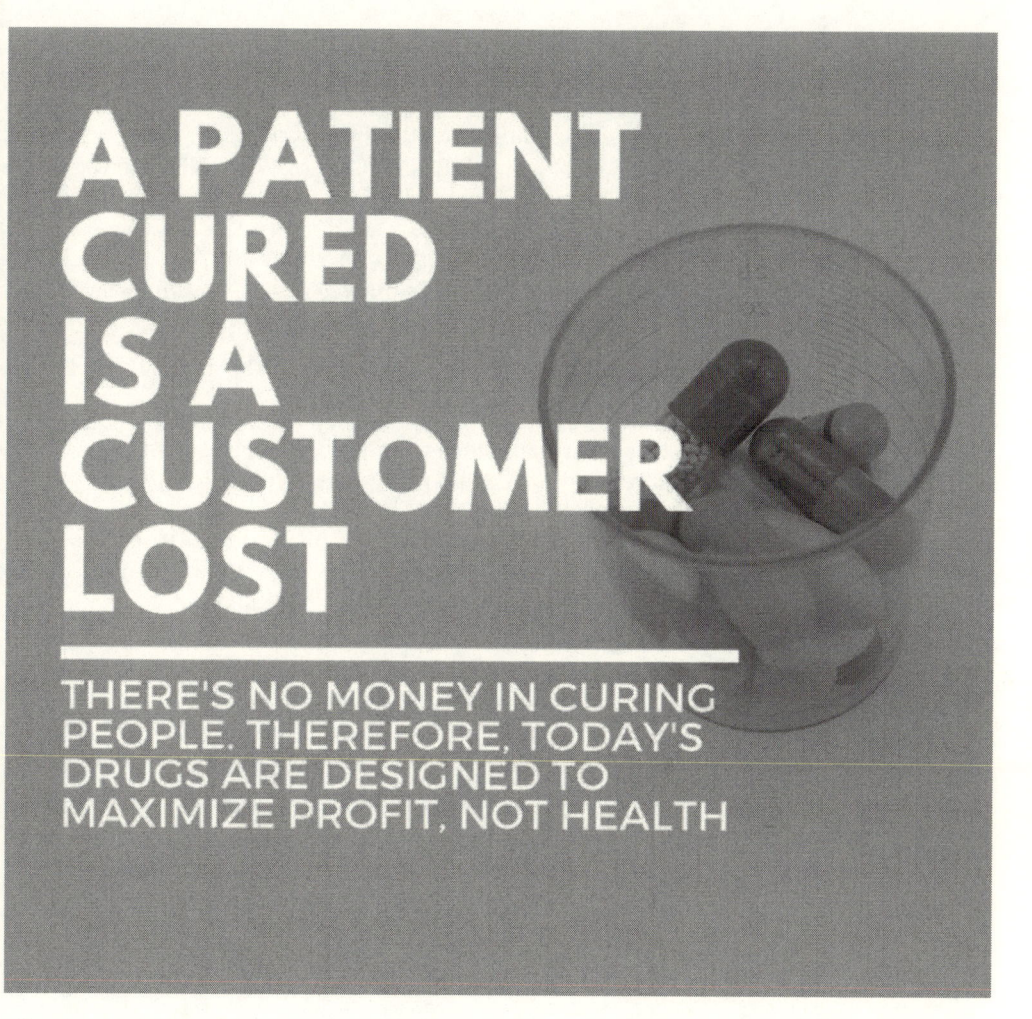

THERE'S NO MONEY IN CURING PEOPLE. THEREFORE, TODAY'S DRUGS ARE DESIGNED TO MAXIMIZE PROFIT, NOT HEALTH

Why are there never any good side effects? Just once I'd like to read a medication bottle that says, "May Cause Extreme Sexiness."

The Medical Trilogy of Terror

But are we totally at fault for getting sucked into this myth regarding medicine and our health? But of course not! Profit from the health industry plays a major role in our overall health and I don't mean that in a good way! Between the **doctors**, **hospitals** and **insurance companies**, we're being lied to, overcharged, misdiagnosed, and over prescribed to death!

We're not the only race that's being affected by this but when you add all of the other things I've talked about that's against us, you'd think that we'd get the hint by now.

The big 3 have strategically managed to manipulate the system, all in the name of profit. And now we have to ask ourselves this, "Is this HEALTHCare or WEALTHCare we're dealing with?

If we knew better would we really do better? I honestly don't think so. We're the same individuals that will go get tested and once we're told that we're sick we simply accept the news, no questions asked, no desire to seek an alternative to surgery, no second opinion! We just accept the death sentence that's handed to us, sit back and wait to die! And when the bill comes, we pay!

Doctors PRACTICE medicine! In order to practice medicine, you need something or someone to practice on! You're practicing in order to get better at your skillset.

These are the same doctors that prescribe you a pill that has more deadly side effects than ingredients in the pill itself! And before you know it, you need to offset your side effects of that pill by being prescribed yet another dangerous pill and it goes on and on and on....

But these pills only MASK the problem, not fix it! Have you ever wondered why other races in other parts of the world don't deal with a fraction of the health issues we have here in the states? That says all that we need to know! Our great-grandparents and grandparents somehow managed to live long and fruitful lives while barely dealing with the issues we deal with today. Ever wondered why? Half of the things we put in our body isn't even considered food! A couple of short, geeky whitecoats are somewhere in some lab creating something that's going to make your food get larger, look brighter in color, taste better! And what those geeky, whitecoats fail to tell us is that this same additive can also be used to clean your car rims!

As you can tell, there's several broken parts in the health industry that only enhance the numerous health issues we struggle with as a people. From diabetes to obesity, doctors to prescriptions drugs, we're in the worse position possible when it comes to health and the black race in an advanced country like America. The answers are there, the resources are available, but like most of the things we've discussed so far in this book, we simply can't seem to get out of our own way!

There are some things in life that's kind enough to offer us a second opportunity, our overall health isn't one of them. There's not a *backup body* sitting in some warehouse at our disposal. This is it people, take care of it and in return it will take care of you!

In Conclusion

The only thing worse than being blind is having sight but no vision.

My prayer for you is that you take a closer look at yourselves, be honest with yourself about how you feel regarding these topics that were discussed in this book. All of us can *talk* about our daily challenges, but it's only when we make a conscious effort to change that mindset through our actions, that we break free from those *internal chains* that hold you and I down.

Other races out there *quietly* see the people from the African descent as "Sleeping Giants". **They know** if this race ever decided to get their act together, it's frightening what we can do collectively as a whole!

They see it and *we feel it*, but we can't seem to get out of our own way long enough in order to achieve it!

And just like a slow leak in a tire, *we choose* to instead stop by the gas station, add some more air (superficial antidotes), instead of taking that tire to the shop to get it *repaired* (talking, seeking answers and working things out with each other).

And as long as we keep adding *air* to our ongoing internal issues, we'll keep struggling the way we do until one day we'll find ourselves on the side of the road, flat, and no spare to help us get back on the road!

Unfortunately, what will be written will be the downfall of the greatest race in what many considered the greatest nation on earth. What will be written will be about the many issues we left unaddressed, issues that led to our slow demise as a people!

The choice is ours.

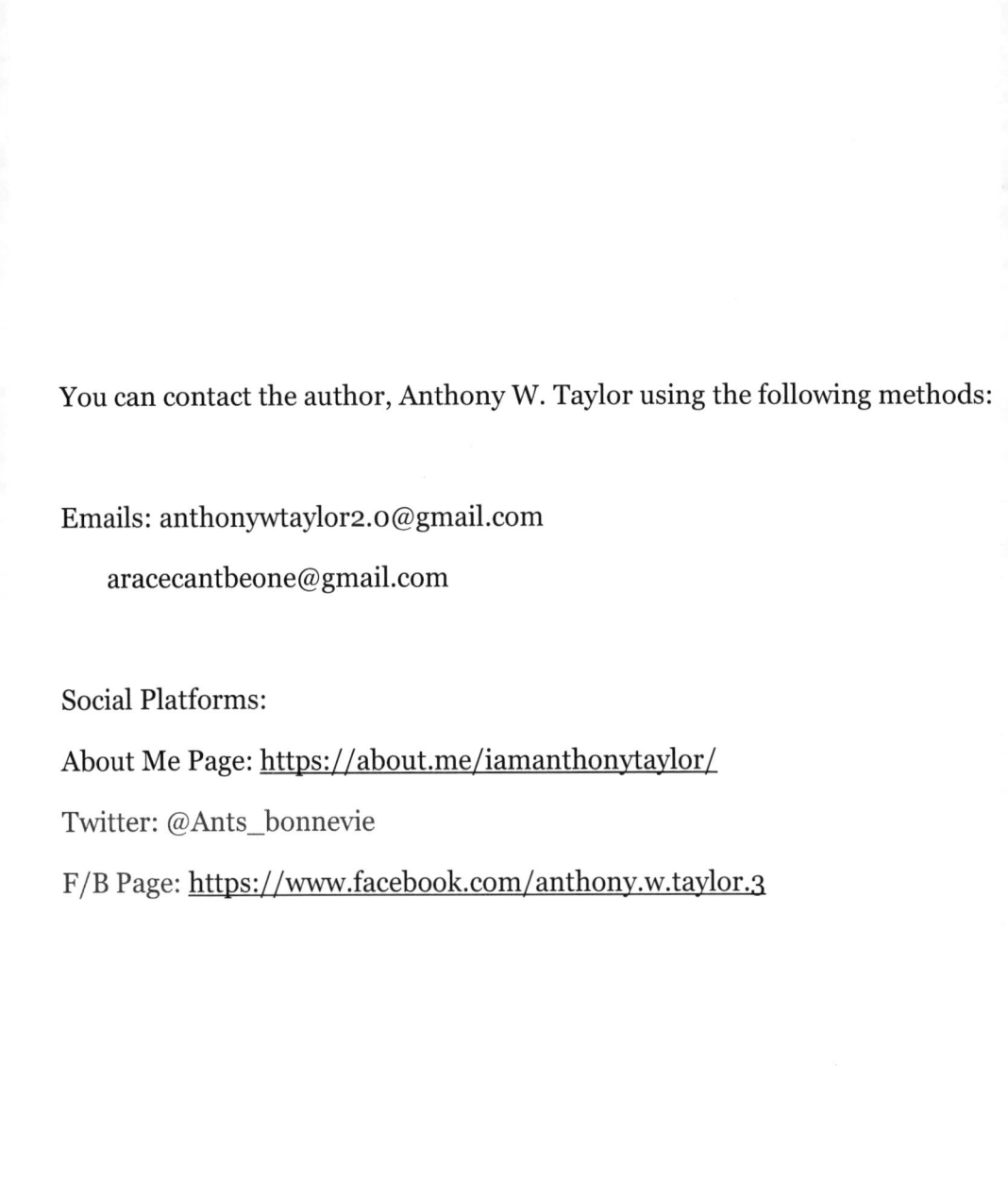

You can contact the author, Anthony W. Taylor using the following methods:

Emails: anthonywtaylor2.0@gmail.com

aracecantbeone@gmail.com

Social Platforms:

About Me Page: https://about.me/iamanthonytaylor/

Twitter: @Ants_bonnevie

F/B Page: https://www.facebook.com/anthony.w.taylor.3

Made in the USA
Middletown, DE
25 April 2024